The Art of War in Ancient Assyria

The Sargonid Dynasty at War from Sargon II to Ashurbanipal (722 – 627 BC)

Roland Sennewald
Stefano Borin (Artwork)

ZEUGHAUS VERLAG GmbH

"And, behold, they shall come with speed swiftly: none shall be weary nor stumble among them; none shall slumber nor sleep; neither shall the girdles of their loins be loosed, nor the latchet of their shoes be broken:
Whose arrows are sharp, and all their bows bent, their horses' hoofs shall be counted like flint, and their wheels like a whirlwind:
Their roaring shall be like a lion, they shall roar like young lions: yea, they shall roar, and lay hold of the prey, and shall carry it away safe, and none shall deliver it"
Isaiah, 5, 27-29

Author: Roland Sennewald
Artwork: Stefano Borin
Map: Karsten Sennewald
Editing (German version): Michel Danhardt
Translated by: Dr. Jan Eschbach
Layout: Stefan Müller

Publisher: Zeughaus Verlag GmbH
                      Knesebeckstr. 88
                      10623 Berlin, Germany
                      Telephone: +49 (0)30/315 700 30
                      Email: info@zeughausverlag.de
                      Website: www.zeughausverlag.de

Translator's note:
The transcription of Assyrian cuneiform characters and other ancient written sources frequently renders different nomenclatures depending on the nationality of the translator. In the given translation of a German work, most Assyrian place and personal names have been adapted to the forms commonly used in English works (for example, the Assyrian king Shalmaneser is commonly called Salmanassar in German works). The translator apologizes for any mistakes or oversights which may have occurred in the process.

Bibliographic information from the Deutsche Bibliothek: The Deutsche Bibliothek lists this publication in the German National Bibliography; detailed bibliographic information is available at http://dnb.ddb.de
Printed in European Union
Originally published in German as *"Die Kriegskunst der Assyrer von Sargon II. bis Assurbanipal"* (Berlin: Zeughaus Verlag, 2022) in the Heere & Waffen series number 41. This edition revised and augmented based on the German original.

© 2022 Zeughaus Verlag GmbH, Berlin, Germany
ISBN: 978-3-96360-049-4

Frontispiece:
Two Assyrian warriors securing booty, c. 714 BC. In the background may be seen an alabaster stone relief from the South-Western Palace of Assyrian king Sennacherib at Nineveh, now at the Pergamonmuseum, Berlin.

CONTENTS

AUTHOR'S NOTE

Thanks is due to the many people who supported me while this book was in the making. I should especially like to thank those who helped me gain access to the numerous pictorial and written sources available at various museums, galleries, and auctioneers all over Europe.

My thanks goes to Lic. phil. Werner Rutishauser, Schaffhausen, Roy Boardman, London, and to Dr. Harald Schulze, Munich.

I am grateful to the staff of auction houses Gorny & Mosch, Munich, and Hermann Historica, Munich; Christoph Bacher, Vienna; the staff of the Badisches Landesmuseum, Karlsruhe; Gerhard Althaus, Weimar.

I should also like to thank my former colleagues Christoph Diehl, Manuel Baistock and Benjamin Brandt, Leipzig.

Thank you to bpk-Bildagentur, akg images, bridgeman images Berlin for providing me with pictorial sources.

Thank you also the the staff of the Vorderasiatisches Museum, Berlin, and to Dr. Campbell Price of Manchester Museum.

Finally, I would like to express my gratitude to my brother Karsten for contributing the maps to this work, and to Michael Danhardt, Munich, for proof-reading. Pride of place surely goes to Stefano Borin, Verona, for his kind and patient cooperation, and his wonderful artwork.

Roland Sennewald

INTRODUCTION

When approaching Assyrian history, one is quickly baffled by the large amount of uncertainties appertaining to this period. Scientific works abound, but then so do the caveats presenting themselves to the reader. Many aspects of the history of ancient Ashur remain annoyingly elusive – words and phrases like *probably, presumably, possibly, it may be assumed that .., surely, might, could, ought to, there is no concrete evidence for* ... may be found in every work covering the period.

Why is this so?

When we deal with the events that determined the rise of the first high civilizations in the Ancient Middle East we must come to terms with the fact that a large proportion of our conclusions must remain guesswork. The sources from this remote time must of necessity remain few and in between. The concept of coherent and continuous historiography was alien to all Middle Eastern cultures of the time. For their research, scholars are mainly dependent on the pictorial depictions of Assyrian kings as they appear on steles, reliefs (orthostates), and palace murals. To these may be added the written source material, mostly in the form of earthen tablets, prisms, relief inscriptions, and dedicatory inscriptio
ns to be found in what has remained of contemporary buildings. Papyri are as yet extremely rare. Some inscriptions relate the military triumphs of the respective monarch who had the building erected. Especially the stone reliefs in the royal palaces at Kalchu (Nimrud), Nineveh (Mossul) and Dur Šarrukin (Khorsabad) display the glorious endeavours of the ruling Assyrian Great Kings. These depictions were instruments of propaganda, with the help of which Assyrian rulers sought to impress and intimidate their subjects, allies, tributaries, enemies, and guests. Other pictorial sources comprise images on archaeological finds such as jewellery, furniture, vases, seals, and others. Only long after the Assyrian Empire had come to ruin were parts of its history incorporated into the works of ancient historians such as Herodotus (490/480 BC – 430/420 BC), and into the Bible's Old Testament. It remains a stroke of good fortune that some buildings rich with inscriptions and reliefs were preserved for centuries in the shifting sands of the Middle Eastern desert.

The 19th century saw the rise of an unprecedented archaeological enthusiasm which prompted individual scholars and devoted laymen to dig up and exploit these valuable sources. In this context, the decoding of Egyptian hieroglyphics as well as Aramaic characters and the Akkadian and Sumerian cuneiforms by a small number of dedicated academics in the course of the 19th century was a valuable asset. These accomplishments set the scene for the comprehension of the written sources.

The era of Mesopotamian high civilization in the fertile crescent between the Euphrates and the Tigris in the first millennium BC was in fact an extremely warlike one. Incessant incursions conducted by nomadic tribes into the rich countryside situated between the two rivers forced the local Assyrian population to develop military countermeasures. At first these were of a purely defensive nature, but as the power of the kings grew, the Assyrians became more aggressive. In the Assyrian heartland, which roughly covered the area of modern Iraq, the course of the 9th century BC witnessed the development of a very effective and highly organized Assyrian military culture. Led by powerful Great Kings,[1] the Neo-Assyrian army was vastly superior to the military forces of its neighbours. The kingdom of Ashur swiftly began to exploit this superiority, aiming to extend and secure its trade routes, specifically to the Mediterranean. Borders were steadily expanded in order to seize economically vital tributes from the conquered neighbouring kingdoms and tribes. A ring of provinces and client states surrounding the Assyrian heartland provided a political and military *cordon sanitaire*.

The most important and memorable episodes of military campaigns, remarkable feats of architecture, and the delivery of tribute payments by foreign emissaries were recorded in stone and set up for all to see in the royal palaces of the Neo-Assyrian kings. Occasional military setbacks were of course discreetly ignored. The stone bas-reliefs not only show Assyrian soldiers and auxiliaries but also their enemies, albeit less frequently. Modern scholars must take into account that the stone masons and sculptors responsible for creating the reliefs concerned probably employed a good degree of idealization. Nevertheless, it is only the temples and palaces of the Egyptian pharaohs of the Middle Kingdom (an era preceding that of the Assyrians by 500 years) which can compete with the abundance and variety of Assyrian triumphal sculpture. Concerning their value regarding the neo-Assyrian Empire, Egyptian pictorial sources are thus only of very limited value. After the fall of Assur, only the Persian royal residences at Persepolis and Susa were capable of creating similar sculptural grandeur.

Even though the transition from the Bronze to the Iron Age was already well under way in Mesopotamia in the first millennium BC, many pieces of Assyrian military equipment and articles of everyday use were still made of bronze. This again is a stroke of luck for modern scholars, since bronze artefacts are far superior to iron when it comes to surviving the ages more or less intact. Small wonder that most of the surviving Assyrian finds in today's museums and private collections are made of bronze.

---

1 The era of the so-called Old Assyrian Empire reached from 1800 to 1380 BC, that of the Middle Assyrian Empire from 1380 to 980 BC. Finally, the time of the Neo-Assyrian Empire has been determined by scholars as lasting from 912 BC to the fall of Nineveh in 612 BC. The Empire continued in its death throes until the fall of Harran in 610. Parts of the Assyrian army seem to have continued the struggle until 605 BC.

During the time of the Neo-Assyrian Empire Assyria reached the apogee of its expansion and political power. The royal Sargonid dynasty[2] (722–627 BC) was instrumental in this era of triumph. Its kings spent their reigns forever on campaign against political usurpers and conquered peoples seeking to regain their independence. Further challenges arose in the form of nomadic incursions and raids by warlike steppe and mountain peoples. Of course these never-ending wars stretching over a period of altogether a century posed a strain on the empire's military, economic and financial resources. Assyria was surrounded by by hostile powers and rivals merely waiting to pounce on the powerful, rich and fertile power in their midst. The Sargonid dynasty effectively succeeded in creating the first true great empire in the history of mankind. At the height of their power, the Great Kings even ruled the huge ancient kingdom of Egypt which in the south reached right down into the area of modern Sudan. The powerhouse of this unprecedented juggernaut was the Assyrian army, an experienced, well-equipped and superbly organized fighting force.

THE SOURCES

In the mid-19th century, interest in the archaeological heritage of Ancient Mesopotamia increased. Excavations were financed and conducted to a large extent by private individuals, many risking their own lives in the process. We are fortunate that photography at this time was still an artistic extravagance rather than a means of documentation so that finds were documented by skilled draughtsmen and almost immediately published. As the sands of Mesopotamia began to yield their long-guarded treasures, scholars were making steady progress decoding Assyrian cuneiform characters.

Who were the men that with their private initiative laid the foundations of our understanding of ancient Assyrian history and culture? Paul-Émile Botta (b. Turin, 6th December 1802, d. Achères/Poissy, 29th March 1870), a doctor, was the consular agent of France in Mossul when he proceeded to excavate the western slope of the Kuyunjik, a hill situated immediately to the north-east of Mossul on the eastern bank of the Tigris. It also stood in the area once occupied by the Assyrian capital of Nineveh. Unsuccessful at first, Botta duly turned his attention to Khorsabad, which was a good 20 kilometres distant. His curiosity aroused after listening to descriptions by local Arabs, he commenced excavations and in 1843 was rewarded by the discovery of the royal palace of King Sargon II, founder of the Sargonid dynasty. Having reported his find to the French government, Botta received a generous financial subsidy to continue his research. In 1844 he was joined by artist Eugène Flandin, who henceforth took the responsibility of making accurate drawings of the finds made.

Flandin's high-quality pictures were published in several volumes in 1849/50. Convinced that he had actually discovered the Assyrian royal capital, Botta named the work *Monument de Ninive*.

Victor Place continued the excavations begun by his fellow countryman at Khorsabad in the years 1852 to 1854. He succeeded in uncovering another 186 rooms of Sargon II's royal residence. He also excavated the so-called *ziggurat*, a massive terraced, pyramidal structure which formed the core of the city's temple complex, as well as several other religious buildings. Place also succeeded in digging up the city walls together with their massive gates. His work was actively supported by Colonel Henry Creswicke Rawlinson, who in his position as Queen Victoria's consul general in Baghdad took considerable interest in the excavations and generously donated several finds to various museums. Misfortune struck briefly when a raft carrying several stone reliefs and plaques with cuneiform inscriptions capsized on the Tigris when hostile Arabs attacked the convoy. Some objects were later recovered and are now on display at the Louvre in Paris. For scientifically accurate documentation of his finds Place now not only relied on draughtsmen but also on a number of photographers. He published his finds in three magnificent vol-

---

2   King Ashurbanipal died in 627 BC (some sources claim he died earlier); whether or not his successors right up the demise of Ashur were members of the same dynasty remains impossible to tell.

Idealized reconstruction of Nimrud

Austen Henry Layard, *The Monuments of Nineveh*, vol. 1 (frontispiece)
Digital library, University of Heidelberg.

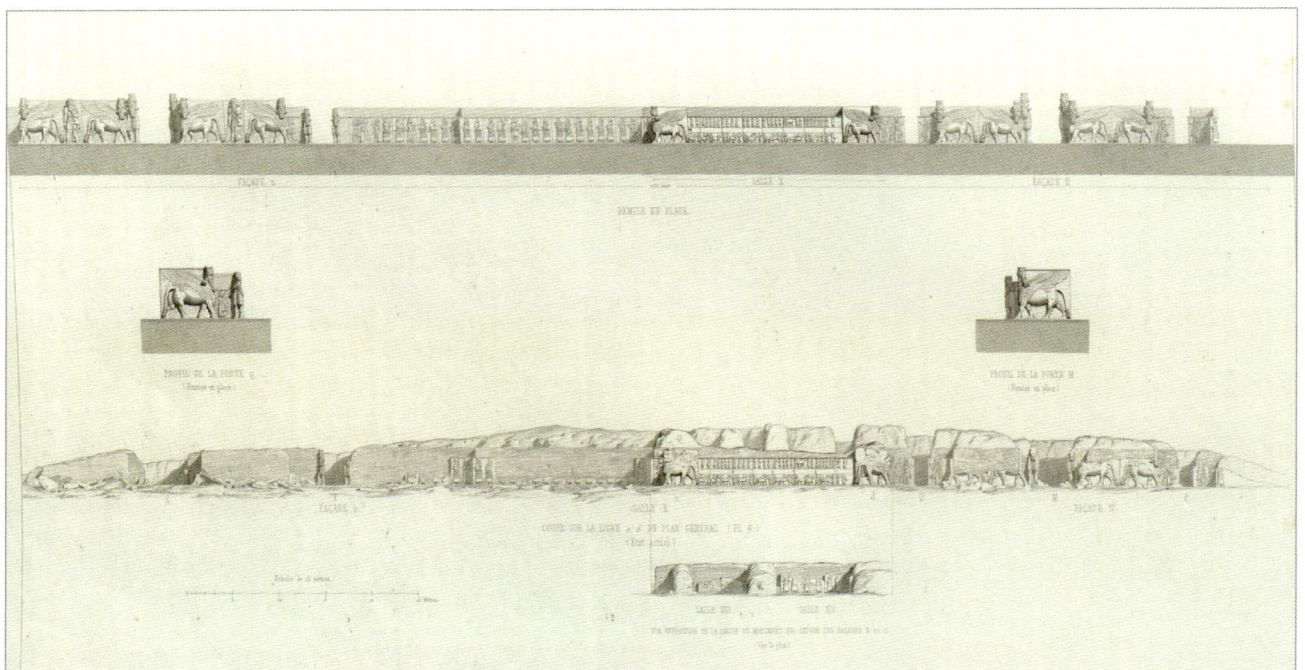

Eugène Flandin's impression of a façade of Sargon II's palace at Khorsabad

Paul-Émile Botta, *Monument de Ninive*, vol. 1 (plate 7, page 14)
Digital library, University of Heidelberg.

Reconstruction of palace interior
Austen Henry Layard, *The Monuments of Nineveh*, vol. 1, plate 2, (page 30).
Digital library, University of Heidelberg.

Another view of a façade of Sargon II's palace at Khorsabad
Paul-Émile Botta, *Monument de Ninive*, vol. 1, plate 30.(page 37).
Digital library, University of Heidelberg.

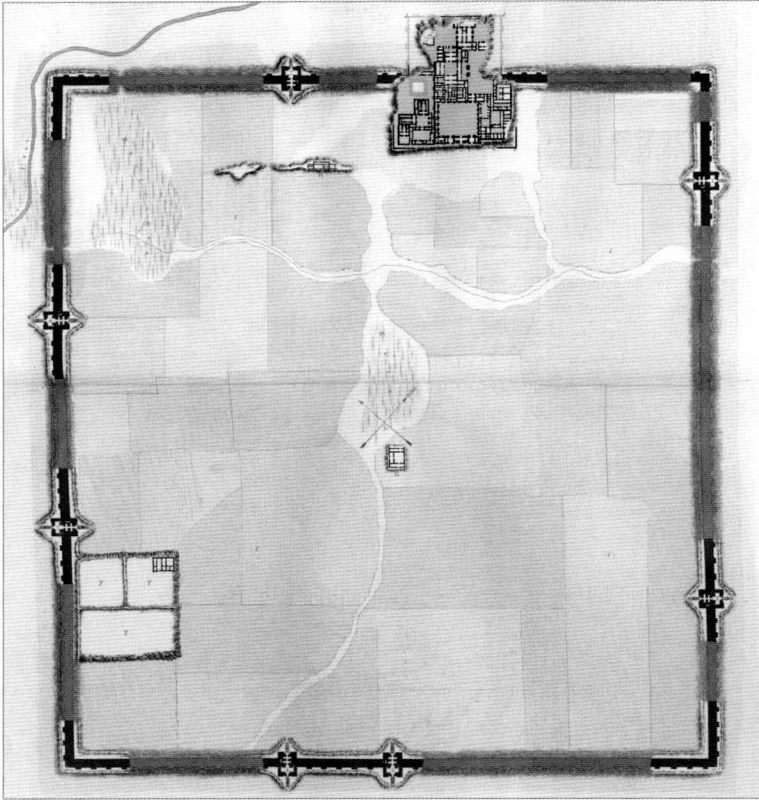

Archaeological layout of Khorsabad

Victor Place, *Ninive et l'Assyrie*, vol. 3 (plates), plate 2 (page 12). Digital library, University of Heidelberg.

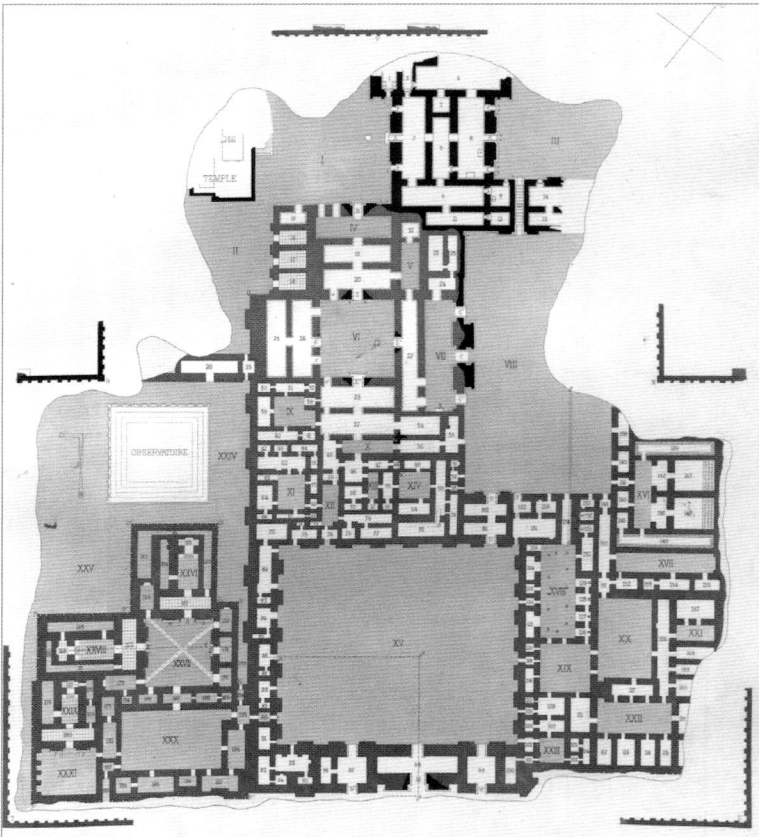

Archaeological layout of the palace of King Sargon II at Khorsabad

Victor Place, *Ninive et l'Assyrie*, vol. 3 (plates), plate 3 (page 13). Digital library, University of Heidelberg.

Reconstruction of Sargon II's palace at Khorsabad by French architect and historian Charles Chipiez

Victor Place, *Ninive et l'Assyrie*, vol. 3 (plates), plate 18 (page 29).
Digital library, University of Heidelberg.

Two reconstructions of gates at Sargon II's palace at Khorsabad

Victor Place, *Ninive et l'Assyrie*, vol. 3 (plates), plates 21 and 24 (page 35).
Digital library, University of Heidelberg.

umes titled *Ninive et l'Assyrie* in the years 1867 to 1870. Botta and Place found a worthy successor in Austen Henry Layard (b. Paris, 5th March 1817, d. London 5th July 1894). This intrepid traveller and adventurer turned archaeologist was a friend of Botta's and excavated at Nimrud and Nineveh, where he too was convinced to have found the ancient Assyrian capital. He unearthed the so-called Northern Palace of Neo-Assyrian monarch Ashurnasirpal II (r. 883-859 BC) with its abundant sculptures and reliefs. Later he also excavated the so-called Central Palace of King Tiglath-Pileser III (745–727 BC), which however proved a disappointment since it yielded only few finds. Tiglath-Pileser III is credited with having founded the Neo-Assyrian standing army. Layard went on to excavate King Esarhaddon's (680–669 BC) South-Western Palace. It turned out that this building had not been completed, which explained its poor state of preservation.

Layard decided to move on. Returning to the previously abandoned Kuyunjik, he promptly discovered King Sennacherib's South-Western Palace. Layard was assisted by his friend Hormuzd Rassam, a local who later became Layard's successor, continuing excavations after Layard had left the Middle East. The ruins of Sennacherib's palace contained some well-preserved reliefs and part of the royal library inscribed on clay tablets. All finds were documented by Layard himself, and by British artists F. C. Cooper and Bell. The drawings were later used in London as templates for copper engravings, which were duly published to make them accessible to both scholars and the public.

Another great archaeological success was the discovery of King Ashurbanipal's Northern Palace resplendent with stone reliefs. A further palace of King Sennacherib's, comprising troop quarters and an arsenal, was found following excavations at a hill in Niniveh named Nebi Yunus. The ruins also yielded a sensational 25, 000 earthen tablets which constituted King Ashurbanipal's royal library. Today they may be found at the British Museum in London, along with the reliefs. Layard's substantial finds were published in two volumes titled *The Monuments of Nineveh* in the years 1849 to 1853 and focused on his excavations at Nimrud and Nineveh.

Another excavator worth mentioning here was William Kennett Loftus who managed to unearth a number of impressive reliefs in the Northern Palace in 1854, depicting Ashurbanipal's famous lion hunt, and a royal banquet. The outbreak of the Crimean War put an end to this series of successful excavations.

In 1880, Hormuzd Rassam excavated the magnificent bronze gate mountings of the Mamu Temple at Imgur-En-lil (modern Balawat) with numerous images from the time of King Shalmaneser III (858–824 BC). Similar gate mountings were found by various scholars in different Assyrian royal residences.

Later excavations conducted by German archaeologists were also successful: Ernst Koldewey's digs brought to light large parts of Ancient Babylon while Ernst Walter Andrae dug up remains at Assur.

In order that we may understand Assyrian history, we must turn to a number of other sources besides the impressive ruins in the desert: for example, pictorial and written sources include the so-called White Obelisk of King Ashurnasipal II (883–859 BC), the Black Obelisk of King Shalmaneser III (858–824 BC) and two prisms from the time of King Sennacherib. Another valuable source has come down to us in form of a stele from the time of Sargon II, discovered at Kition on the island of Cyprus.

The White Obelisk is an object made of limestone adorned with bas-reliefs which was found at Nineveh. It is now in the British Museum. At first scholars were unsure as to the time of its creation. However, parallels between inscriptions on the obelisk and the annals of Assurnasipal II. confirm that that the monument can be dated to the early reign of this monarch.

The artistic execution of the Black Obelisk, also to be found at the British Museum, is stylistically quite similar to that of the White Obelisk. The obelisk was hewn out of the black limestone commonly found in Nimrud in northern Iraq. It was found at Nimrud in 1846 by Austen Henry Layard. The obelisk is covered with altogether 20 bas-reliefs, every one of its four sides displaying five friezes each. They depict five kings paying tribute to Shalmaneser III and expressing their submission by prostrating themselves in front of the king. They have been identified as Sua of Gilzanu from north-western Iran; Jehu, ruler of Israel's northern kingdom; the King of Muški; Marduk-apil-uşur of Šuhi from the middle Euphrates region, and Qalparunda of Patina (the future Antioch). Comments composed in cuneiform provide explanations of the events depicted.

Of the two prisms recording the deeds of King Sennacherib, the so-called Taylor Prism[3] is in the collection of te British Museum. It was excavated at Nebi Yunus and has been dated to the year 691 BC. The prism of burnt clay relates Sennacherib's first three western military campaigns against Syria and Palestine, during which the king's generals besieged (or rather, blockaded) the city of Jerusalem.

The second prism can today be found at the Oriental Institute of the University of Chicago. It was found at the Kuyunjik. It was made in the year 689 BC and records details from King Sennacherib's first two military campaigns. An extended version of these reports was discovered in-

---

3   The prism was purchased at an antique market in Nineveh in 1830 by Colonel Taylor, British ambassador to Baghdad. It later came into the possession of the British Museum

scribed on two monumental bull statues at Nineveh dating from 694/693 BC. The inscriptions relate the events of Sennacherib's first six campaigns.

Together with the above, a cylinder discovered by Hormuzd Rassam relating the campaigns between 703 and 701 BC along with a large number of individual clay tablets form the brunt of the written sources available about this era in Assyrian history. The Sargon stele, a damaged basalt stone, was discovered buried in rubble in a garden in the village of Kition near Larnaka on the island of Cyprus in autumn 1835. It later found its way into the collection of the Preußisches Museum in Berlin and is now on display at the Pergamonmuseum, Berlin. The stele celebrates Sargon II's victory over the seven kingdoms of the island of Ia (i. e. Cyprus).

A similar stele commemorating the victories of King Esarhaddon is in the collection of the Vorderasiatisches Museum in Berlin. The basalt stele was found in 1888 at Sama'al (modern Zinjirli) by German archaeologists Felix von Luschan and Robert Koldewey. It measures 3, 18 metres and was made around the year 669 BC. It celebrates Asarhaddon's victories over Pharaoh Taharqa and Prince Abdi-Milkutti of Sidon in the year 670 BC. The sides show the king's sons Ashurbanipal and Shamash-shum-ukin in Assyrian and Babylonian royal regalia.

To these pictorial sources can be added a large number of other reliefs and inscriptions. Like Babylonian, the Assyrian language was essentially a dialect variant of Akkadian, a semitic language now extinct which was itself strongly related to Sumerian.

Following double spread:

King Sargon II, Prince Sennacherib and *Turtānu* general officer.

Reliefs excavated by Botta at Khorsabad (Dur Šarrukin) repeatedly show Sargon II during court ceremonies. He is frequently accompanied by crown prince Sennacherib and high-ranking court officials. The plate depicts the Great King together with his heir and a general. All wear court dress including the traditional shawl draped around the torso. The garments are decorated with fringes and golden applications. The Great King is wearing his distinct royal headdress, the *tiara*. According to depictions on stone reliefs, the *tiara* was also worn on campaign, but it is highly improbable that it was also worn in battle. The crown prince wears a diadem also frequently depicted on stone reliefs. It was probably made of leather with attached golden ornaments. The leather of the sandals was dyed in different colours, as traces of paint found on stone reliefs have shown. Both Prince Sennacherib and the general officer carry maces. Whether these objects actually served as a badge of rank remains unclear. The officer is carrying ceremonial arms in the form of a sword, a bow and a quiver richly decorated with gold. His bronze helmet is modelled on a specimen once in the collection of the Museum of Venice (Giancarlo Ligabue collection). The cheekguards have been added. The helmet is decorated with ornamental grooves and engraved with images of Assyrian deities and other religious motives. These images are surrounded by ornamental beading terminating in animal heads. Lions, bulls, rams and snakes were popular with Assyrian artisans.

All three figures wear precious robes made of fine linen or silk and dyed with purple and indigo. The alabaster façade in the background is modelled on the entrance to the royal palace at Khorsabad. The *Lamassu* (hybrid creatures consisting of winged bull's bodies with human heads) were protective entities warding off evil, and heavenly guardians of the king's royal residence. Their stone images outside palace gates were commonly several metres in height.

THE SARGONID DYNASTY

Following several Neo-Assyrian rulers of varying importance, the Sargonid dynasty came to power in 722 BC. Just how exactly its founder Sargon II assumed royal power remains unclear. There is reason to believe that he succeeded his brother to the throne, but this is merely educated guesswork.[4] The zenith of Neo-Assyrian power was short-lived, the demise setting in under Sargon's great-grandson Ashurbanipal.

In contrast to what is generally perceived, Assyrian rulers were not simply savage warriors wreaking havoc and destruction upon their enemies, but also highly cultivated patrons of architecture and urban development. Magnificent palaces, temples and cities were built under their rule; especially Sennacherib was instrumental in creating an irrigation and public water supply system of aqueducts and canals altogether 240 kilometres in length. This alone constituted a massive technological feat at the time. Sennacherib succeeded in providing his capital of Nineveh as well as its surrounding countryside with a stable and technically reliable water supply from the mountains, which led to the city's considerable growth and helped secure large crop yields; thus famine and ensuing domestic unrest were effectively prevented. The canals were large enough to enable ships to travel on them, facilitating trade and transport. Long before the Roman Empire, an Assyrian ruler created the first aqueducts in history.

---

4   Assyrian kings had the right to nominate their successors, and these were commonly either sons or brothers. There was no right of primogeniture. This circumstance gave rise to many a court intrigue, especially amongst influential concubines and mothers in the ruler's harem.

King Ashurnasirpal II surrounded by courtiers and deities
Austen Henry Layard, *The Monuments of Nineveh*, plate 5 (page 33).
Digital library, University of Heidelberg.

The picture shows a relief from the Northern Palace of Ashurnasirpal II at Nimrud (Kalḫu in ancient Assyrian). Claiming power from the gods, Assyrian rulers frequently had themselves depicted alongside deities. The relief further shows members of the king's personal retinue. They may be eunuchs, guardsmen or royal princes.

Adad-nīrārī II	911–891 BC	Adad-Nirari II
Tukultī-Ninurta II	890–884 BC	Tukulti Ninurta II
Aššur-nâṣir-apli II	883–859 BC	Ashurnasirpal
Salmānu-ašarēd III	858–824 BC	Shalmaneser III
Šamši-Adad V	823–811 BC	Shamsi-Adad V
Adad-nīrārī III	810–783 BC	Adad-Nirari III
Salmānu-ašarēd IV	782–773 BC	Shalmaneser IV
Aššur-dan III	772–755 BC	Ashur-Dan III
Aššur-nirari V	754–745 BC	Ashur-Nirari V
Tukulti-apil-Ešarra III	744–726 BC	Tiglath-Pileser III (also first Assyrian king of Babylon)
Salmānu-ašarēd V	726–722 BC	Shalmaneser V

The Sargonid dynasty

Šarru-kīn II	722–705 BC	Sargon II
Sîn-aḫḫe-eriba	705–680 BC	Sennacherib
Aššur-aḫḫe-iddina	680–669 BC	Esarhaddon
Aššur-bāni-apli	669–627 BC	Ashurbanipal [5]
Aššur-etil-ilani	627 BC	Ashur-etil-ilani
General Sîn-šumu-līšir	627/626 BC	This ruler was not a member of the dynasty. His reign was only brief.
Sîn-šarru-iškun	627/626–612 BC	Sin-shar-ishkun was probably a son of Ashurbanipal. He was killed in the battle for Nineveh.
Aššur-uballiṭ II	612–610 BC	Ashur-uballit II was probably his predecessor's *turtānu* (commander-in-chief of the Assyrian army), or even his brother. He was able to defend the final Assyrian stronghold of Harran against the Medes and Babylonians before being killed in battle. Harran held out until 610 BC.

---

5   The exact year of Ashurbanipal's death is unknown. The last written sources from his reign can be dated to the year 631 BC.

Left page:

Stele celebrating Esarhaddon's victory over Egypt after 671 BC

Vorderasiatisches Museum, Staatliche Museen Berlin; photograph by Olaf M. Teßmer

The stele from the palace at Zinjirli depicts the Assyrian king towering over the defeated pharaoh and one of his allies, presumably Prince Balu of Tyre.

Right page:

Top:

Sargon II attended by two eunuchs

Drawing by Eugène Flandin, Paul-Émile Botta, *Monuments de Ninive*, vol. 2, plate 105 (page 25). Digital library, University of Heidelberg.

Below left:

King Ashurbanipal on campaign

Austen Henry Layard, *The Monuments of Nineveh*, plate 72 (page 101).Digital library, University of Heidelberg.

From the palace at Nineveh (Kuyunjik), the relief shows the king in his chariot accompanied by his driver and an attendant holding a parasol. At top right an archer draws his bow protected by a shield bearer.

Below right:

Sargon II conversing with a dignitary

Drawing by Eugène Flandin, Paul-Émile Botta, *Monuments de Ninive*, vol. 2, plate 105 (page 25). Digital library, University of Heidelberg.

Plate 71. The King returning from Battle (Kouyunjik)

King Ashurbanipal and retainers on a lion hunt

Victor Place, *Ninive et l'Assyrie*, vol. 3, plate 53 (page 69).
Digital library, University of Heidelberg.

ASSYRIAN POLITICAL AND RELIGIOUS CENTRES

In the long course of Assyrian history, kings changed their official places of residence several times. In spite of this, the original royal residence of Ashur remained the empire's religious centre.

The city of Ashur was founded ca. 2700 BC.
Not only did it become the Assyrian Empire's cultural and religious hub, it was also an important focal point of trade along the Tigris. At the end of the 19th century BC Shamsi-Adad I laid the foundations of the first Assyrian Empire.

13th century BC
The city of Kar-Tukulti-Ninurta briefly becomes royal residence. Shortly afterwards however, King Tikulti-Ninurta I once again makes Ashur the official capital of the empire.

883–859 BC
King Ashurnasirpal II makes Kalchu (Nimrud) his official capital.

722–705 BC
King Sargon II moves the capital to Dur-Šarrukin ("Fortress of Sargon"/Khorsabad).

705–682 BC
King Sennacherib makes Nineveh the capital of the Assyrian Empire. Nineveh remains the capital until the empire's fall in 612 BC. Ashur falls to the Medes in 614 BC and is completely destroyed. After the fall of Nineveh, Harran becomes the final Assyrian capital until 610 BC.

THE NEO-ASSYRIAN EMPIRE'S NEIGHBOURS

Who were the peoples and empires continuously engaged in both trade and conflict with their Assyrian neighbours? The formerly rich and powerful Hittites, Mitanni, and Sea People were no longer of any profound political or military significance. The Hittite Empire had crumbled torn by internal strife, very possibly under the onslaught of of the Sea Peoples (among them the Philistines) and Kaskians, in the 12th century BC. Remains of the Hittite Empire had managed to survive into Neo-Assyrian times in the form of small city states and princedoms in Northern Syria. These political entities had to rely on alliances in times of conflict since they were far too weak to provide for themselves against the great military powers of the day. With permission from the Egyptians, the Sea Peoples had settled in the Nile Delta and the south-eastern Mediterranean in the 12th century BC. Having mingled with the local population, those settling in the north were later referred to as the Phoenicians. The settlers on the Mediterranean coast, who had mixed with indigenous Semitic and Canaanite peoples, no longer posed any serious military threat. These small kingdoms and city states were thus of negligible economic and political influence on a wider scale. Their economies were based chiefly on local agriculture, craftsmanship, and trade by land and sea.

Nevertheless, the Assyrians found themselves faced with a number of formidable enemies: the Egyptian rulers of the 24th and 25th dynasties with their powerful armies supported by Nubian, Greek and Libyan auxiliaries, the Israelites, Cimmerians, Scythians, Cilicians, Chaldeans, Babylonians, Arameans, and the smaller kingdoms based in the northern and north-eastern mountainous regions such as the Manneans and, above all, the Medes, Urarteans and Elamites. Especially the latter two rose to considerable power in the final phase of the Neo-Assyrian era, and under strong rulers significantly influenced political and military affairs in the region between 750 and 627 BC. The kingdom of Elam to the southwest and Urartu in the north were continuously involved in a series of interminable conflicts with the Assyrian Empire. The kingdom of Urartu, which was situated in what is today Armenia, eastern Turkey and northern Iran, had developed a high degree of political, military and administrative efficiency and as such exercised a fair amount of influence on its Assyrian neighbours. Urartu had developed a consider-

Sennacherib at Lachish in Judah
Austen Henry Layard, *A Second Series of Monuments of Nineveh*, plate 23 (page 37).
Digital library, University of Heidelberg.

able edge especially in the fields of horse breeding and metallurgy. After a series of hard-fought campaigns in which both powers sought to secure the trade routes to the Mediterranean, a lasting status quo was finally established from which both sides drew cultural and political profit. The Urarteans adopted cuneiform script.

The Assyrians proved unable to either destroy or subdue the kingdom of Urartu due to its geographical position. Mountainous terrain, roads which proved difficult to negotiate for an invader, well-designed and strategically well-placed fortresses, and a highly organized army all secured Urartu's independence and survival. Urartu even managed to outlive the Assyrian Empire for a while until it too succumbed to the attacks of the Scythians and Medes. The Elamites, the Assyrians' powerful and implacable enemies to the southeast, were finally conquered by Ashurbanipal only after a series of prolonged and costly campaigns lasting several decades. The early Sargonids succeeded in subduing the semitic northern kingdom of Israel, while the southern kingdom of Judah survived until conquered by the Babylonians after the fall of the Assyrian Empire.

Especially the festering conflict with Babylonia, a kingdom with a longer history and a rich cultural heritage older than that of Assyria, remained the focus of Assyrian policy for many decades. Indeed, both cultures were inseparably linked by common origins and cultural roots. Nevertheless, the Babylonian élite was fiercely independent and sought to maintain its self-determination by forging a series of alliances designed to keep the troublesome Assyrians at bay. The Assyrians attempted to counter these moves by establishing kings from their own royal dynasty on the throne of Babylon, or by exercising indirect power in the form of client kings; yet even these proved a source of never-ending politcal turmoil in the region.

Another ancient political power with which the Assyrians were forced to contend was Egypt. The pharaohs sought to secure their age-old influence in Palestine and Syria and consequently clashed repeatedly with Assyrian political and military expansion. Several campaigns saw Assyrian armies penetrate deep into Egyptian territory, some even reaching as far as Nubia in modern Sudanese regions.

The Assyrians were not interested in conquering foreign territory as an end in itself. Their foreign policy revolved around the idea of protecting the Assyrian heartland by a string of provinces ruled by Assyrian governors. These in turn were to be surrounded by allied nations which were expected to recognize Assyrian supremacy and pay tribute to the Great King. Their rulers were vassals obliged to support the Assyrian army with military and financial aid in times of war. Otherwise they were more or less left to do as they pleased. If however they attempted to regain their independence or disrupted vital trade connections, they risked severe retaliation that might result in their deposition and their kingdom being turned into another Assyrian province. Vassals who dared to turn upon their Assyrian masters were frequently subjected to appalling punishments which served as a deterrent to others.

In the wake of conquest or the suppression of revolt the Assyrians frequently deported a region's élite along with a certain proportion of the population and resettled them in other parts of the empire with the aim of intermixing them with the local populace. Deportations often involved resettlement in regions a great distance away from a people's native lands. This brutal policy resulted in large-scale regional ethnic cleansing, the depopulated lands being resettled with Assyrians or members of previously conquered peoples. The idea behind these measures was to disrupt ethnic and political homogeneity in specific regions and thus prevent the potential of large-scale and widespread opposition against Assyrian rule. A welcome side effect was the concentration of artisans' know-how and industrial expertise in the core regions of the empire. Another pillar of Assyrian foreign policy was a balanced system of alliances, not infrequently bolstered by carefully negotiated marriages. Children and other close relatives of allies and client rulers served as hostages, living a life of luxury at the Great King's royal court. In order to prevent palace coups, conspiracies and political intrigue, the Great Kings regularly appointed eunuchs to serve in high-ranking positions, e. g. as provincial governors or military commanders. For obvious reasons, these men were comparatively uninterested in amassing long-ranging political power and influence.

A concise overview of kingdoms, city states and princedoms bordering on the Assyrian Empire[6]

Sources frequently mention places, ethnic groups and countries which today can no longer be clearly defined or located. Even those peoples and states known to us were undergoing a series of political and geographical changes during the 8th and 7th centuries BC so that often it remains impossible for the modern scholar to determine the exact whereabouts and size of minor kingdoms, princedoms and city states of the time.

Kingdoms[7]

Urartu
Egypt (including Nubia and Libya)
Babylonia
Elam
Israel (Northern Kingdom)
Israel (Kingdom of Judah)
Lydia
Aribi (Arab kingdom)
Cyprus
Edom
Moab
Ammon
Phrygia

The large number of petty kingdoms comprised Hamath, Zirkirtu, Karullu, Anzan, Arza, Melid, Gurgum, Kadesh, Damascus, Karkemish, Aram, Hubushkia, and many more.

Nomad tribes

Chaldeans[8]
Arameans[9]
Arabs
Cimmerians
Scythians
Persians
Medes[10]
Zagros mountain tribes (Hillakki, Audia, Namri, Gambulu)

City states and princedoms[11]

Phoenicia (city states of Sidon, Arwad, Byblos, Akko, Ushu, Tyre, Gebal, Samsimuruna)
Philistines[12] (Ashkelon, Ekron, Gath, Gaza, Ashdod, Joppa, Benebarqa, Altaqu, Timath)
Aramean-Chaldean princedoms (e. g. Bit Agusi (Arpad), Bit Amukani (Chaldea), Bit Yakin, it Adini (Til-Barsip), Bit Gabbari (Sam'al), Bit Ammana)
Mannaea
Ellipi
Cappadocian princedoms (Miliddu, Tabal)
Cilician princedoms (Quwê and Tarsis)
Mushki
Subria
Muşaşir
Syrian petty states (Damascus)

---

6 This overview is by no means complete and merely mentions the most important powers.

7 There is no clear-cut distinction possible between kingdoms and mere princedoms at this time since many minor rulers stylized themselves as kings and were frequently addressed as such.

8 The Chaldeans primarily inhabited the region of southern Mesopotamia.

9 The Aramean tribes mostly inhabited northern Syria and founded several small princedoms in the area. They were most probably related with the Chaldeans.

10 Persians and Medes are first mentioned in Assyrian sources around the year 835 BC.

11 The population of these city states and their immediate surroundings constituted an ethnic mix as a result of frequent migrations in previous centuries.

12 The Philistine city league or confederation was a result of the Sea Peoples' migratory wave. The Egyptian pharaohs had granted the newcomers permission for permanent settlement in return for military support. The Shardana (or Sherden) people were prized auxiliaries in the Egyptian army.

Black Sea

Cimmerians

Urart

Lake
Van

Supria

Hubushkia

Dur-Sl

Tabal

Melid

Kummuh

Harran

Phrygia

Gurgum

Karkemish

Til-Barsip

Chabur

Lydia

Quwê

Sam'al

Cilicia

Euphrat

Hamath

Arwad

Byblos

Sidon

Damascus

Tyre

Samaria

Israel

Ammon

Ashdod

Ashkelon

Jerusalem

Lachish

Mediterranean Sea

Gaza

Judah

Moab

Edom

Sais

Memphis

Re

**Map of the Assyrian Empire and
its neighbours under the Sargonids
in ca. 700 BC**

Karsten Sennewald, 2021

Theben

Caspian Sea

Scythians

Lake Urmia

Gilzanu

Muşaşir   Zikirtu

Arbela

Mannea

Upper Zab

Allabria

Medes

kin

Lower Zab

Karullu

Luristan

Kalchu

Arrapha

Parsua

Ellipi

Assur

Gambulu

Elam

Tigris

Susa

Persians

Ural

Babylon

Bit Yakin

Uruk   Ur

Persian Gulf

THE SARGONIDS

Author´s note: *Assyrian campaigns are dated according to the date of the Assyrian New Year. Thus, one and the same campaign may be referred to as two separate campaigns if it extended beyond the end of any one year.*

Sargon II (r. 722–705 BC)

Sargon II founded a new dynasty which was to strongly influence the history of the Neo-Assyrian (or late Assyrian) Empire. Especially thanks to the reforms of his predecessor Tiglath-Pileser III the Assyrian army had at this stage reached a completely new quality in terms of organisation and efficiency. It is highly probable that Sargon II usurped his royal power from his brother. In the course of his reign he made Khorsabad (Dur Šarrukin, the "Fortress of Sargon") his royal capital and embellished it with a large number of palaces and other buildings which had not been completed by his death. Nimrud, his predecessors' capital, sank to the status of a provincial town and never regained prominence.

Exactly how Sargon assumed power is still largely a matter of conjecture, but he seems to have been a brother of Great King Shalmaneser V and thus a son of Tiglath-Pileser III. He seized power in the course of a putsch which probably occurred during Shalmaneser's siege of Samaria in 722 BC. The Great King was assassinated, but there is no evidence that despite being its prime beneficiary Sargon was himself part of the conspiracy.

Sargon had served as his brother's general in several campaigns, one of them against the kingdom of Israel [13]and its ruler Hosea. Both brothers claimed the credit for the victory. The siege of Samaria lasted three years, and the city fell into Assyrian hands in January 722 BC. The city's fall does not seem to have served any profound tactical purpose however, since Shalmaneser V had already conquered the surrounding countryside and taken King Hosea prisoner. A large part of the Israelite population was deported in accordance with Assyrian policy, surviving units of the Israelite army were incorporated into the Assyrian forces. This also was common practice. Foreign contingents of Assyria's armed forces can be recognized by their appearance and armament on palace reliefs. In this case, Israel was obliged to provide 50 chariots for Sargon's army.

The campaigns of Sargon II

❐ 722 BC: Victorious campaign against Israel. This terminates the 300-year existence of the Northern Kingdom of the Jews. Large parts of the Israelite nobility and social élite are deported to other parts of the Assyrian Empire. Assyrian province of Samerina founded.

❐ 721 BC: Chaldean prince Merodach-Baladan allies himself with the Elamites under King Humban-nikash I and crowns himself King of Babylon. Sargon is in no position to tolerate this. The event marks the beginning of a prolonged conflict over control of Babylonia. The ensuing battle of Dur-ilu ends in a draw. This is followed by a decade of warfare as both sides grapple with each other for control of Babylonia.

❐ 720 BC: A revolt in Syria led by Princes Hanno of Gaza and Yahubidi of Hamath is crushed. Yahubidi is defeated in battle at Karkar on Hamath territory. Samarian Israelites seem to have supported the insurrection. An Egyptian army under Pharaoh Shabaka moving in support of the Syrian rebels is defeated by Assyrian forces to the south of Gaza outside the town of Raphia. Hanno of Gaza is taken prisoner, the city of Raphia is razed to the ground and its population deported. Syria and Palestine are now firmly under the Assyrian yoke. Repeated Egyptian attempts to regain influence in the region culminate in Assyrian invasion of Egypt several decades later. Sargon is now free to turn his attention elsewhere. He proceeds to reconquer several kingdoms in Northern Syria and the Taurus mountains extending into western Media, who have chosen to throw in their lot with the Kingdom of Urartu, before marching against Urartu itself. In the course of the same year an Assyrian army suffers defeat against the Elamites at the battle of Der.

13　After the death of King Solomon, the Kingdom of Israel was divided into the Northern Kingdom of Israel with its capital of Samaria, and the Southern Kingdom of Judah with its capital of Jerusalem.

Assyrian forces besiege a town

Austen Henry Layard, *The Monuments of Nineveh*, plate 78 (page 107). Digital library, University of Heidelberg.

This scene shows the variety of the soldiers' equipment. Note the double teams of archers and spearmen carrying large wicker paveses.

❑ 719 BC: The Empire's northern border with Urartu sees fighting between Assyrian troops and the forces of princes Iranzi of Mannaea and Metatti of Zirkirtu. Assyrians under Sargon take and sack cities of Suandahul[14] and Durdukka. The cities of Sukia[15], Bala and Abitikna are occupied, the populations deported to Syria.

❑ 718 BC: Campaign in Tabal (province of Cappadocia in modern Turkey) against Kitakki of Sinuhtu. Assyrians turn their attention west.

❑ 717 BC: Assyrian victory over city state of Karkemish (or Carchemish) under its ruler Pisiris. Karkemish is the last surviving stronghold of the former Hittite Empire. The city and its surroundings are made an Assyrian province. At the same time, Assyrians establish strongpoints along Egyptian border to guard against Egyptian attacks. Egyptian pharaoh moves against Assyrians and gives battle at Wadi Al-Arish south of Gaza. This suggests that apart from the royal army another Assyrian army has taken the field, presumably under the command of a *turtānu* or one of the royal princes. A revolt of the cities of Papa and Lallukna on the Urartean border is suppressed.

❑ 716 BC: Successful campaign against Ellipi in the territory of modern Iran (Media). Assyrians defeat Mannaeans and several other rebellious princes along the Urartean border. The country of Karalla is conquered and subdued.

❑ 715 BC: Assyrians campaign in Urartean frontier region (Namri, Sangibutu, Bit-Abdani). As a result, Sargon II receives tribute from 45 Median tribal leaders. The same year sees Assyrians campaigning against Arab tribes in the south. Again, this campaign seems to have been conducted by a second Assyrian force commanded by a provincial governor. Victory against Prince Mita of Mushki in the region of Tyre (Phoenicia).

❑ 714 BC: Sargon II takes the field against Urarteans under their king Rusas I and his allies. Sargon himself has allied himself with Mannaean prince Ullusunu, who rules the region south of Lake Urmi. Mannaean princes allied with Urartu are defeated and subdued. Assyrians lay waste to Urartean southern ter-

---

14   The names of numerous towns and cities have become almost impossible to determine exactly. This is due to varying transcriptions and translations from the original cuneiform inscriptions. Spelling in this work has been adopted from the respective secondary sources.

15   Assessing the size and strategic importance of cities mentioned in inscriptions is often pure guesswork. Most were presumably fortified settlements with populations of several thousand.

ritories. Sargon wins battle against Rusas I at Mount Uaush (or Waush; presumably modern Mount Simirra in western Iran). Assyrians owe victory largely to heavy Urartean losses sustained in previous fighting against Cimmerian nomads in the western Caucasus. It may be supposed that the Assyrians take deliberate advantage of the Urarteans' predicament. Owing to the efficiency of their intelligence service established and headed by crown prince Sennacherib, the Assyrians are able to exploit Urartean weakness, pursuing their own ends to the best of their abilities. The campaign against Urartu in 714 BC is arguably one of the most well-documented military events in Assyrian history. Sources are comparatively plentiful and coherent. German archaeologists were able to excavate tablets with cuneiform inscriptions [16] giving a detailed description of the campaign. Sargon had the events recorded in writing to give an account of himself and his deeds to the god Ashur at the temple of Ashur, where they were eventually discovered. The tablets are a rich source for the military historian and have entered historiography under the name of *Letter to Assur* (German: *Gottesbrief*). On the way back from his victorious campaign Sargon has his troops ransack the city of Mushashir (Mušašir) with its magnificent temples to Urartean god Haldi. King Rusas I feels so deeply at this humiliation that he allegedly commits suicide. Nevertheless, he appears very much alive in Assyrian accounts of later campaigns. Sargon takes great pains over his enumeration of the booty seized at Mushashir – the sack of the city is depicted on the walls of his palace at Dur-Sharrukin, from where Eugène Flandin eventually copied it into his sketchbook.

❏ 713 BC: Victorious Assyrian campaign against Prince Amaris of Tabal, an ally of Urartu. Amaris is captured and taken to Assyria. A revolt in the province of Karalla is put down.

❏ 712 BC: Assyrians defeat Tarhunazi of Melid, a rebellious princedom in Cappadocia. Melid becomes part of the new Assyrian province of Tel-Garimmu. During peace negotiations, Sargon II receives 2 000 bronze shields as tribute.

❏ 711 BC: Successful campaign against the rebellious ruler of the Hatti state of Kurkuma (Gurgum). A small crack Assyrian force is sufficient to quell the revolt. A revolt in Palestine is crushed by a *turtānu*. The land of the Philistines [17] becomes part of the province of Ashdod. This includes the five cities (*pentagon*) of Ashkelon, Ekron, Gath, Gaza, and Ashdod. The Kingdom of Judah and the people of Edom and Moab are severely chastised for their participation in the rebellion.

❏ 710/709 BC: Assyrians campaign against Babylon under usurper Merodach-Baladan (Marduk-apla-iddina II) and Chaldaeans. Chaldean-Aramean tribes are defeated and subdued. The ancient cities of Ur, Erech, Irid, Durilu, Larsa, Kisik and Kulunu are occupied by Assyrian troops. Merodach is driven from Babylon.

❏ 709 BC: Prince Muttallu of Kummuh rebels against Assyrians. An Assyrian army sent against him causes him to flee. His family is captured, his treasures confiscated. His land is annexed and made an Assyrian province.

❏ 709–707 BC: Seven Cypriot kingdoms (Assyrian: Jatnan) voluntarily submit to Assyrian rule. A stele is erected at Kition to commemorate the occasion. It mentions several other campaigns of Sargon II at the time. An Assyrian governor successfully leads his army across the Taurus mountains into Asia Minor. He defeats Prince Mita of Mushki, who had taken up arms against Sargon II, and lays waste to the lands under his rule.

❏ 708 BC: The Assyrians march against Prince Nibe of Ellipi who has allied himself with Elam. Assyrians defeat Elamite auxiliaries. The capital of Ellipi, Marubishti, is taken and Nibe's brother Ispabara installed as king.

❏ 705 BC: The Assyrian army seems to have been ambushed campaigning against the princedom of Tabal. Sargon II is killed. His body is never recovered. He is the first Neo-Assyrian monarch not to receive burial in the Old Palace at Ashur – this is regarded as an unprecedented calamity.

---

16 Most of these tablets are now in the collection of the Louvre in Paris and the Pergamonmuseum in Berlin.

17 The Philistines were an ethnic group which formed part of the Sea Peoples migrating into the Levant from the northern Mediterranean in the 12th century BC. They clashed on various occasions with Egyptian, Canaanite, Israelite and Hittite forces. Other groups of the Sea Peoples presumably had their origins in Sardinia, Sicily and Crete, which may explain their differing outward appearances on Egyptian reliefs.

Sennacherib 745–680 BC (r. 705–680)

Sennacherib followed his father on the throne after the latter's death in 705 BC. He moved the Assyrian capital from Khorsabad to Nineveh.[18] Parts of Nineveh's palaces were excavated by Austen Henry Layard and Hormuzd Rassam from under the hills of Kuyunjik and Nebi Yunus. The hill of Kuyunjik to the north yielded the ruins of Sennacherib's South-Western Palace and the Northern Palace of Ashurbanipal. The ancient South-Western Palace had been restored according to Sennacherib's wishes. South of Nineveh the hill of Nebi Yunus yielded the so-called Rear Palace or Review Palace, which primarily served as an armoury and military barracks. Reliefs in the South-Western Palace show campaigns of Sennacherib and vanquished leaders offering tribute to the Great King. Some reliefs also concern themselves with the victories of Sennacherib's grandson Ashurbanipal, who inhabited the palace before the completion of the Northern Palace, which he undertook to completely rebuild. Most reliefs about Ashurbanipal's exploits were situated in the Northern Palace, but this was only completed in 646 BC. Among the finds discovered in this building was a large part of Ashurbanipal's famous library of clay tablets, which provides historians with invaluable information not just on Assyrian history but the history of the entire Mesopotamian region at the time. Ashurbanipal had the new Northern Palace erected where the old Northern Palace (Bit-Reduti) had once stood, the place where his father Esarhaddon had spent most of his childhood. The Sargonid dynasty thus replaced two ancient palaces in Nineveh with new ones. Sennacherib fortified the city, whose walls eventually reached a total length of 12 kilometres. The ancient traveller accessed the capital through one of its eighteen gates.

The campaigns of Sennacherib

After his father's death Sennacherib was forced to fight a lengthy campaign against an alliance of Elam and Babylon, which was still striving to preserve its independence. Individual Chaldean rulers also joined the alliance. Sources about the first two years of Sennacherib's reign are scarce, but despite campaigns in other regions it was especially the conflict with Elam and Babylon[19] on which the new king's attention and generalship were focused.

❏ 704 BC: Assyrians campaign against the Kulumeans.

❏ 703 BC: A Babylonian revolt is crushed. Sennacherib wins battle of Kish (Kuta) near Babylon against Chaldean prince Merodach-Baladan who has still not given up his claims to the throne of Babylon. He is able to raise an army of Chaldeans, Elamites and Aramean tribal levies. The Assyrian army pillages the territory of the Bit Yakin tribe and terrorizes the local population. Merodach-Baladan escapes and continues to stir up trouble against Assyrian power in the region.

❏ 702 BC: Sennacherib leads campaign against the Kassite tribes in the Zagros mountains. The army occupies strategically important local settlements. All occupied territory is added to Assyrian province of Arrapcha. Another campaign in the same year leads to the conquest of Ellipi, a region on the south-western border with Media. Its ruler Ispabara is expelled. Ellipi is divided, parts becoming an Assyrian province.

❏ 701 BC: The princes of Sidon, Tyre and Ashkelon, and King Hezekia of Judah rebel against Assyrian rule. Sennacherib leads his army into Syria and moves south along the Mediterranean coast towards Sidon. King Luli of Sidon flees at the Assyrian army's approach. Kings[20] Abdiliati of Arwad, Urumilki of Byblos, Mitinti of Ashdod, Jorom of Edom, and Minechem of Samsimuruna are frightened into submission and hurriedly renew their alliance with Assyria. The kings of Amurru follow suit. The rulers of Ashkelon and Judah are determined to continue the struggle however. King Hezekia of Judah has captured King Padi of Ekron, who has remained loyal to Sennacherib. The Assyrian army defeats the forces of King Zideqa of Ashkelon and proceeds to lay siege to Jerusalem, locking the rebellious Judaean king into his capital "like a bird in a cage," as Sennacherib himself grimly

---

19   The power of Babylon was not restricted to the city of the same name, but comprised an entire region also referred to as Babylonia.

20   Assyrian sources indiscriminately tend to call even petty rulers ‚kings'. To distinguish them and their comparatively small political influence from that of the Assyrians, Assyrian rulers are referred to as Great Kings.

---

18   Nineveh was situated in the immediate vicinity of today's city of Mossul east of the Tigris. Its ruins were buried beneath several hills in the area.

puts it. The Assyrians are however forced to raise the siege due to new troubles on the Babylonian front. Other historians attribute the Assyrians' failure to take Jerusalem to an outbreak of an unknown pandemic. King Hezekia nevertheless chooses to take no further chances and submits to Assyrian rule. In the course of savage fighting around Jerusalem the Assyrians meanwhile have managed to capture 46 towns and fortresses (among them Lachish), which they place in the care of local rulers. The siege and surrender of Lachish is documented by a series of reliefs in Nineveh's South-Western Palace. Even though the Assyrian army excelled at sieges, they were not popular. Losses inflicted by enemy action and disease tended to be high. A mass grave excavated at Lachish yielded the bodies of no less than 1,500 Assyrian soldiers. The King of Judah is forced to pay dearly for his impetuousness: numerous members of the royal house are deported by the victors, along with a large part of the populace and a huge amount of livestock. 30 talents[21] of gold and 300 talents of silver are seized for the Assyrian royal treasury. Large areas of land are given to Ashdod, Ekron and Gaza, who have managed to change sides in time to convince the Great King of their loyalty. The Kingdom of Judah is reduced to Jerusalem and its immediate surroundings. King Padi is freed by the Assyrians and reinstated into his old realm. King Hezekia is forced to acknowledge Assyrian suzerainty and pays tribute to Sennacherib. The rebels had been supported by Egypt under its pharaoh Taharqa[22]. An Egyptian army is intercepted by Assyrian forces under Sennacherib at Altaqu (Eltekeh) in Judah, and defeated. Several Egyptian princes, an Arab general and numerous Nubian charioteers are captured. In the year 701 BC Sennacherib boasts of commanding an army of 185,000 soldiers. The Assyrians incorporate large numbers of former Phoenician, Judaean, Egyptian and Nubian soldiers into their army: 10,000 archers and 10,000 shield bearers are recruited from amongst the prisoners of war. At the end of the year 700 BC Sennacherib is forced to leave the Mediterranean theatre of war to the care of his generals and again turn his attention to the Babylonian troubles: King Bel-ibni, himself Sennacherib's creature on the throne of Babylonia, is trying to break away from his Assyrian overlord with assistance from abroad. He is defeated in battle outside Babylon and captured. Sennacherib now puts his own son Ashurnadin-shumi on the throne of Babylon and sets off to fight the rebel's Chaldean allies.

❏ 699 or 698 BC: Sennacherib's fifth campaign takes him to the mountains of southern Armenia, to the east of Cizre on the upper Tigris. The fighting against the local nomadic mountain tribes is arduous and vicious. The Assyrians' objective is to prevent further nomad incursions into the cultivated plains.

❏ 697 BC: Several minor rebellions in southern Babylonia, e. g. in Nippur and Ukku on the border with Elam, are suppressed.

❏ 696–695 BC: Ionian pirates invade Assyrian provinces of Cilicia[23] and Tabal. These "Gurdi" (Greeks) are eventually defeated with heavy Assyrian losses.

❏ 694/693 BC: Sennacherib's sixth campaign is preceded by brilliant logistical planning. Having commissioned the building of transport ships at Nineveh and Til Barsip, Sennacherib sails downriver to the Persian Gulf and delivers a surprise attack on the Elamite princedom of Nagitu, where Merodach-Baladan, recently escaped Babylonian pretender, has made himself king. A large part of the Bit Yakin tribe lately expelled from its native land by an Assyrian punitive expedition (s. above) has settled in the region. This poses a constant threat for Assyrian security in the area. Merodach-Baladan has still not abandoned his claims to the Babylonian throne and is supported in his political ambitions by the Elamites. Not wishing to provoke Elamite retaliation by invading their territory and fearing the dangers of leading an army through mountainous territory, Sennacherib decides to kill two birds with one stone. Relying on the expertise of the Phoenician and Ionian shipwrights and sailors, the Assyrian fleet sails down the Euphrates and Tigris to the Persian Gulf. At Bab Salimeti on the Euphrates, the troops disembark and link up with Assyrian troops who have arrived via land routes. A riptide floods the army's camp however, forcing the Assyrians to take refuge on board their ships, where they wait for five days for the waters to recede. Despite his tactical stroke of genius, Sennacherib's maritime expedition fails to catch the enemy off guard. The Assyrians disembark their ships at the Ulai estuary in the face of heavy resistance from an assembled enemy force. The Assyrian attack resembles a swarm of locusts and finally succeeds in driving the enemy off. The surrounding countryside is pillaged, settlements are torched and the populace deported. Despite Assyrian attempts to track him down, Merodach-Baladan once again escapes to fight another day. While Sennacherib is busy fighting in the south, his ally King Hallushu-Inshushinak (Ḫallušu-Inšušinak) of Elam rises against

---

21 At the time, one talent amounted to roughly the weight one single man was capable of carrying.

22 Pharaoh Taharqa was of Nubian descent. Nubia was a country situated mainly in modern Ethiopia and Sudan. The Nubians had seized political power in Egypt in the year 746 BC.

23 The Assyrian sources mention the word *gurdi* in the context of the fighting in Cilicia. Ioian Greeks also seem to have been employed as mercenaries.

Assyrian warriors besieging Lachish during Sennacherib's campaign
Austen Henry Layard, *The Monuments of Nineveh*, plate 20 (page 34)
Digital library, University of Heidelberg.

The city's defenders are being subjected to a relentless hail of missiles from the Assyrian archers and slingers. The relief shows a variety of costumes and hairstyles, and different types of Assyrian helmets and shields. Some of the besiegers do not appear to be Assyrians but foreign auxiliaries.

him. He invades Babylonia, takes Sennacherib's son prisoner and instals Babylonian princeling Nergal-Usherib (Nergal-ušēzib) on the throne. Large parts of the country around Babylon are controlled by the rebels, including the town of Nippur. In order to meet this renewed threat, Sennacherib divides his forces and marches north. Ordering his *turtānu*, possibly his brother Sin-ahhe-usur, to retake Babylon, he defeats the Elamites in battle and drives them back across the border. Another battle is fought outside Nippur, in which Nergal-Usherib is defeated and captured. He is brought to Nineveh, where Sennacherib has him "tied to the palace gate like a pig". King Hallushu-Inshushinak is assassinated shortly afterwards.

❏ 693 BC: Taking advantiage of the inner unrest following the king's assassination, Sennacherib invades Elam. He meets with little resistance. The Assyrians lay waste to the countryside and advance to Madaktu. An early winter eventually causes them to turn back and cross the border back into Assyrian territory in 692 BC. The Assyrian invasion sparks off a military conflict between the two neighbouring rival powers.

❏ 692/691 BC: The priests and the people put Chaldean prince Musherib-Marduk (Mušēzib-Marduk) on the throne of Babylon. A sworn enemy of Assyria, the new king allies himself with the new Elamite king Umman-menanu (Humban-nimena according to Walter Hinz[24]). His other allies include several Chaldean rulers, a number of Aramean and Persian tribes, the princes of Anzan (Susiana) and Ellipi, and cities in the Persian Gulf region led by Merodach-Baladan's son.

24 The names of the Elamite kings have been adopted from the work of Walter Hinz, who up to now has published the only German work on Elamite history.

The enemy force assembles at Akkad. Battle is joined at Halule on the Tigris. While Sennacherib's account of the battle as inscribed on the Taylor prism presents us with a resounding Assyrian victory, the battle seems to have ended in a draw. Neither Sennacherib nor his enemies are able to resume the initiative in its wake. Losses on both sides must have been staggering. The Assyrians manage to capture several high-ranking enemies, and several enemy leaders are killed in the fighting. Sennacherib blames the winter cold for the Assyrian retreat. Musherib-Marduk is able to hold his position in Babylon for another three years. His own account of the battle mentions heavy Assyrian losses. Persian mercenaries are mentioned as forming part of the Elamite forces. The Persians had begun to settle in the eastern Elamite princedom of Anzan and would henceforth begin to threaten this kingdom from the east.

❑ 690 BC: Sennacherib campaigns against Arab tribes whose incursions from the south have become a nuisance. Assyrian forces capture the fortress of Adumutu (Adumu) and take the Arabian queen Iskallatu prisoner.

❑ 689 BC: Assyrians sack Babylon in response to the preceding treacheries and political intrigues. Sennacherib is also driven by the lust for personal revenge: in the course of the previous war, his eldest son Ashur-nadim-shumi, whom he had instated as king of Babylon, was taken to Elam by the rebels and executed. After the destruction of Babylon, Sennacherib's hopes of diverting the ancient Babylonian trade routes to Nineveh are more or less brought to nothing.

The following years of Sennacherib's rule remain largely opaque due to a lack of reliable sources. The king is assassinated in January 681 BC probably as a result of a court intrigue headed by two of his sons.[25] The roots of the conflict seem to lie with Sennacherib's choice of his son Esarhaddon as his successor. Only after a brief civil war is he able to assume royal power with the army's support. The campaign against his brothers lasts six weeks. At the battle of Malatya, most enemy troops defect to him. His brothers and their supporters flee to Assyria's old enemy Urartu. Their fates are lost to us. Esarhaddon immediately sets about honouring his father's heritage by embarking on further conquest.

Esarhaddon (r. 680 – 669 BC)

Nineveh remained the Assyrian capital under this king's rule, Esarhaddon choosing to reside in his father's palace. He had another palace in Nimrud, where he turned the palace of Shalmaneser III (858–824 BC) into a fortress and arsenal ("Fort Shalmaneser")[26]. Austen Henry Layard discovered another palace at Nimrud, Ashurnasirpal II's (883–859 BC) so-called North-Western Palace, which was probably also inhabited by Esarhaddon. Layard also excavated Tiglath-Pileser's (744–727) main palace, which was richly adorned with stone bas-reliefs. The walls of Fort Shalmaneser were richly decorated with painted murals and glazed tiles.

In Nineveh Layard was able to excavate another armoury from underneath the hill of Nebi Yunus. It was probably built by Sennacherib but continued in use during his son's reign. The sources tell us that it was custom for the king to inspect the royal arsenals in the first month of the year. The number of horses, mules, donkeys and camels was carefully recorded, as was the number of captives serving in the fortress.

In 2017 Iraqi forces reconquered Mossul from IS terrorists. A tunnel system was discovered which had been used by the Islamists for the illegal trafficking of archaeological finds. But it is an ill wind… archaeologists accompanying the Iraqi army discovered traces of a palace as yet undiscovered which may have belonged to King Esarhaddon. The results of this new discovery are yet to be published. Our knowledge about the reign of Esarhaddon is derived chiefly from rock inscriptions at Nahr al-Kalib near Beirut, a number of reliefs at Nimrud, a stele[27] excavated at Zinjirli (the former Sam'al), and several prisms with cuneiform inscriptions discovered at Til Barsip. Another source are the Babylonian Chronicles, which have come down to us in several versions. The Zinjirli stele shows Esarhaddon receiving the submission of several enemies, among them Pharaoh Taharqa[28] of Egypt and the ruler of Sidon, Abdi-Milkutti[29]. The other side of the stele depicts Esarhaddon's son Ashurbanipal and his elder brother Shamash-shum-ukin (Šamaš-šuma-ukin), who later became king of Babylon. Esarhaddon devoted himself to rebuilding the city after its destruction at the hands of his father. In doing so, he attempted to create an independent power hub for his older son and thus to preserve his loyalty to his chosen successor, Shamash's younger brother Ashurbanipal. It was important for the Assyrians to keep the eternal rival Babylon with its important religious centre, the Esaĝila temple sacred to the god Marduk along with its famous tower,

---

26 Both the palace and the fortress were erected by Shalmaneser III.

27 The stele is now on display at the Pergamonmuseum in Berlin.

28 Some scholars claim that the Egyptian figure is actually Taharqa's son, the crown prince Usanahuru, since Taharqa himself was not captured.

29 Some historians believe that this figure actually depicts Prince Balu of Tyre.

---

25 Some sources refer to only one son instigating his father's murder. Esarhaddon claims that it was in fact two of his brothers, Arda-Mulissu and Nabu-Shar-Usur, who headed the conspiracy. This claim can be found inscribed on a prism fragment.

the Etemenanki, firmly under control. This measure was later to prove a wise and far-sighted move.

The sources listed above are insufficient if we turn to them for information on Esarhaddon's military campaigns. Due to poor health the king frequently seems to have relied on a *rab šāqê* (Rab-Shakeh; vizier or field marshal) to lead his armies, and the provincial governors to lead their contingents independently to contain incursions into Assyrian territory. Cuneiform inscriptions mention the king's habit of turning to the weather god Adad for heavenly advice whether a proposed campaign was promising or not. Esarhaddon's prayers to Adad mention the *rab šāqê* Nabusarusur (Nâbû-šar-uṣur). This officer later served as *rab mūgi*[30] leading another Assyrian campaign in the king's absence.

The campaigns of Esarhaddon

❏ 680 BC: Campaign against Nabu-zer-kitti-lishir (Nabû-zēr-kitti-līšir), son of Merodach-Baladan and prince of Bit Yakin. The prince had rebelled against Assyrian suzerainty and attacked the city of Ur. Esarhaddon does not seem to have led his army in person. He himself writes that he "despatched [his] officers and governors to the border of [Nabu-zer-kitti-lishir's] country". The prince flees to Elam at the Assyrian army's approach; he is assassinated shortly thereafter. A second campaign defeats and subdues prince Bel-Iqisha of Gambulu.

❏ 679 BC: A campaign against the Cimmerians[31] under their king Theušpa (Teushpa) ends in victory at Hubusna. An Assyrian army marches against the Hillakki tribe in the mountains along the Tabal border. Prince Asuchili, ruler of Arza, is captured and brought to Nineveh in chains. There the unfortunate prince is put on display alongside a bear and a dog. A third campaign defeats the Cimmerian Parnacaean tribe. The Mannaeans and Cimmerians are likewise brought to heel.

❏ 679/678 BC: Prince Hazailis of Arza is defeated by Assyrian forces. Assyrians campaign against Arabs.

❏ 678 BC: Assyrians capture Chaldean prince of Bit-Dakuri Shamash-ibni, who had seized power in Babylon. He is brought to Assyria and executed.

❏ 677 BC: After rebelling against Assyrian rule, the city of Sidon is taken and sacked. The population is deported to the Assyrian heartland. The faithless vassal king of Sidon Abdi-Milkutti and his ally, Cilician prince Sanduarri, are captured and executed. The Sidonian nobles responsible for the city's rising are paraded through the streets of Nineveh with the severed heads of their rulers dangling from their necks. Sidon becomes an Assyrian province. Esarhaddon commissions the building of a new city close to Sidon which he names "Esarhaddon's fortress", or "Esarhaddon's harbour" in his honour.

❏ 677 or 676 BC: Campaign in the Taurus mountains. Several Median cities are conquered and subdued. Another campaign leads Assyrian forces to Patusarra, a region settled by Persians and Medians situated between the Bikni mountains (comprising Mount Demavand) and the north Persian salt flats.

❏ 676 BC: Another Assyrian campaign in the Taurus mountains is brought to a successful conclusion. Assyrians are also forced to repulse Mannaean and Median incursions on northern and eastern borders. Assyrians campaign as far as modern Tehran region. A chain of fortresses is erected in the Zagros mountains to protect the Assyrian Empire's eastern border.

❏ 675 BC: Assyrian army takes the field against Mugallu of Melid (Meliddu) and the Chaldean Bit-Dakuri tribe. Melid is unsuccessfully besieged in 675 BC. Assyrians repel Elamite attack on the city of Sippar. Assyrians invade Bazu, which the sources refer to as a parched and salty plain. The campaign is probably directed against nomads roaming the Syrian desert around Damascus. The small town of Arzania (Arza?) is captured.

❏ 674 BC: A first Assyrian campaign against Pharaoh Taharqa ends in failure, the Assyrians presumably suffering a defeat at the Egyptian border. Led by high-ranking officials, the Assyrian army campaigns against the Aramean kingdom of Bit-Amukani in southern Mesopotamia in the same year.

❏ 673 BC: Successful Assyrian campaign against Subria (Šupria) to the northwest of Assyria, where political enemies of the king had taken refuge. The local ruler had refused to hand them over to Esarhaddon, who decides to invade. Another Assyrian objective is to recapture slaves who had escaped across the Assyrian border. In his account of events inscribed on a clay tablet, Esarhaddon proudly claims to have integrated numerous prisoners of war into the Assyrian army: "...and I chose warriors hardened in fighting and battle and made them my royal troops". The Assyrians

---

30   *Rab šāqê* can also be translated as "royal cup bearer". This makes sense, since high-ranking court officials were commonly trusted with high military positions. *Rab mūgi* translates roughly as "commander-in-chief".

31   The Assyrians were compelled to amost incessant warfare in the north, where the so-called Umman-Mandu („horde") consisting of Cimmerians, Scythians and Parnacaeans continuously raided the frontiers.

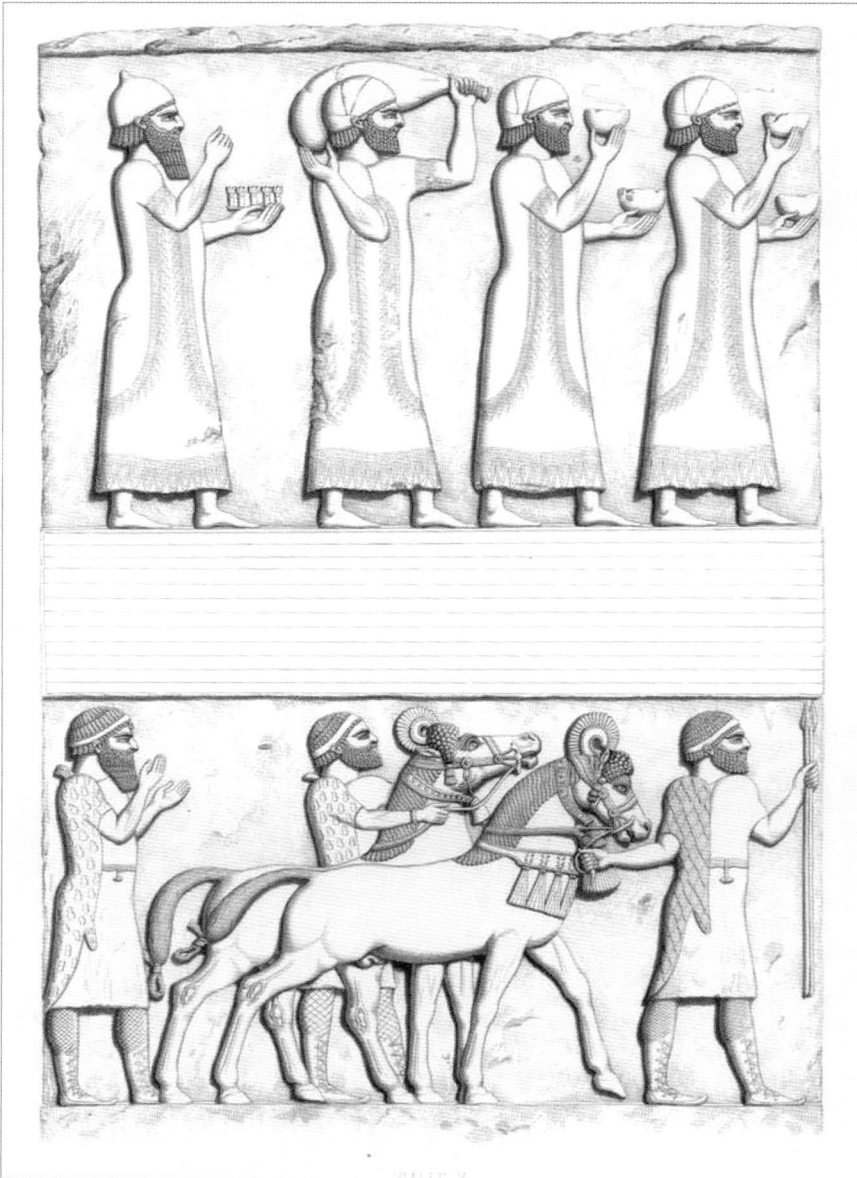

Foreign emissaries pay tribute

Paul-Émile Botta, *Monument de Ninive*, vol. 2, plate 48 (page 126). Digital library, University of Heidelberg.

This double relief shows envoys from two different subject nations paying tribute to Sargon II. The lower relief shows a people evidently skilled in horse-breeding, possibly the Urarteans, Mannaeans, or Median nomads.

recruit charioteers, horsemen and infantry, but also various engineers and artificers into the army. Some of the slaves the Assyrians have managed to recapture are mutilated as a deterrent, the remaining number are restored to their former owners. The Assyrians also capture a number of Urarteans who had fled to Subria as political enemies of the king. These are promptly handed over to Urartu. Both powers are interested in maintaining a stable status quo at this time. The Assyrians lay siege to Ubbume, the capital of Subria; other Subrian towns are captured without difficultiy. Ubbume is situated on a high precipice, which forces the Assyrians to construct a siege ramp of earth, timber and stones in order to reach the walls. The Subrians attempt to set fire to the Assyrian siege engines by employing naphta, but the breeze drives the flames back towards their own defences. Ubbume is taken, the majority of the local population deported. Esarhaddon distributes most of the spoils among his troops, who according to his own words "..are always at my side and dispatch my enemies." Subria becomes an Assyrian province. Assyrian losses are light: in his account to the god Ashur, Esarhaddon proudly claims that he only lost one charioteer, two cavalrymen, and three engineers.

❒ 672 BC: The sources record no military campaign in this year.

Assyrians besiege a Phoenician city

Austen Henry Layard, *The Monuments of Nineveh*, plate 65 (page 95).
Digital library, University of Heidelberg.

The relief was found at Ashurbanipal II's Northern Palace at Nimrud. The relief depicts several events taking place. The defenders manning the walls are identifiable as Phoenicians by their headdresses. Their beards and hairstyles resemble those of the Assyrians. The Assyrians are attempting to to break down the gates and walls while the defenders throw rocks and shoot their bows at the besiegers.

❑ 671 BC: Second Egyptian campaign. On their way, the Assyrians depose prince Balu of Tyre, who has defected to the Egyptians. Before he is able to invade Egypt, Esarhaddon faces the combined armies of 22 Palestinian kings, among them Manasseh of Judah. The Assyrians are victorious at the battle of Ashkelon. The second Egyptian campaign is meticulously planned. Arabs support Assyrian logistics by providing camels to carry the army's water supplies. This enables Assyrians to circumvent the Egyptian frontier fortresses. The Nile delta is swiftly brought under Assyrian control, the army then marches south fighting a running battle with retreating Kushite forces. Esarhaddon claims that "five times I struck the enemy with the deadly tips of my arrows." After 15 days of forced marching Assyrians reach and storm the Egyptian capital of Memphis. In his account of the campaign Esarhaddon repeatedly mentions the use of chariots, which thanks to the terrain the Assyrians are able to put to good use. Pharaoh Taharqa retires to Upper Egypt and decides to bide his time. Meanwhile the Assyrians capture most of the Egyptian royal family (including the crown prince) along with doctors, artisans (chariot builders), astrologers and many other skilled craftsmen. They are deported to Assyria. Esarhaddon is careful to mention the large amount of horses and chariots captured from the enemy. Numerous Egyptian charioteers, horsemen, archers and shield bearers are recruited into the Assyrian army. Esarhaddon places 22 Egyptian nomes under the rule of local princes supervised by Assyrian officials.

❐ 670 BC: Several attempts are made by Assyrian generals and nobles to depose Esarhaddon and his designated successor. The revolts are crushed, the ringleaders are brought to justice.

❐ 669 BC: The Egyptian campaign is renewed after Pharaoh Taharqa has allied himself with several local princes and mounted a counter-offensive. Historians presume that the Egyptian forces were able to advance to the Nile delta. On the way to rejoining his troops, Esarhaddon dies at Harran. His son Ashurbanipal succeeds him and manages to bring the campaign to a successful conclusion. Assyrians win battle of Shupri and two other engagements. Memphis falls after a brief siege.

Ashurbanipal (r. 669–627)

Ashurbanipal ruled the Assyrian Empire from October 669 BC to 627 BC. Esarhaddon's second son, he was not at first designated his successor, but was eventually chosen as his father's heir. This was partly due to his grandmother Naqia's political talent, who managed to promote her Babylonian family line at the Assyrian court. Ashurbanipal was the last in the line of Assyria's great rulers. His brother Shamash-shum-ukin was crowned king of Babylon at his father's instigation. Ashurbanipal had a new Northern Palace erected on the Kuyunjik and resided in his grandfather's South-Western Palace until the new building was completed. The old Northern Palace had become derelict over time so that the new building had become necessary.The new palace was erected on the site of the former palace of Bit Reduti, in which Ashurbanipal had resided as crown prince.

Some events thematized on bas-reliefs
at Ashurbanipal's Northern Palace:

Conquest of Babylon	(648 BC)
Conquest of Hamanu in Elam	(647 BC)
Conquest of Thebes	(664/663 BC)
Lion Hunt	

Some events thematized on bas-reliefs
in the Southern Palace:

The Battle on the Ulai River	(655 BC)
Sennacherib's conquest of Lachish	(701 BC)

Another source regarding Ashurbanipal's campaigns is the so-called Rassam cylinder.

The campaigns of Ashurbanipal

Several sources covering Ashurbanipal's reign and miitary campaigns have survived. From these we may deduce that the Great King did not always assume personal command of his armies, preferring to appoint a *turtānu* to take charge. Due to a lack of reliable source material, providing exact dates for all of Ashurbanipal's military undertakings is as yet impossible. Some dates must therefore remain conjectural:

❐ 668 BC: On a cylinder, Ashurbanipal records his third campaign against King Ba'al of Tyre. It is not implausible that he was already involved in commanding an Assyrian force against Ba'al as crown prince under his father Sennacherib in 671 BC. It is also possible that Ba'al ventured a second revolt against his Assyrian overlords in 668 BC. Exploiting any confusion arising from a change of rulers abroad for one's own ends was common political practice at the time. At any rate, it seems to have taken only a short siege for Tyre to back down and return to the Assyrian fold. The Babylonian chronicles also mention an Assyrian campaign against Elam in the same year. The Elamite province of Kirbit seems to have been the origin of frequent raids into Babylonian territory. A combined Assyrian and Babylonian army commanded by a vizier conquers the troublesome province and deports the population to Egypt.

❐ 667/666 BC: A *turtānu* leads Assyrian forces on a campaign against Pharaoh Taharqa, who proceeding from Nubia and Upper Egypt has reconquered parts of his former realm. The Assyrians choose a double approach, one force invading on land while the other lands in the Nile Delta after sailing the Mediterranean. The Assyrians are supported by 22 client kings from Cyprus and the Levant. Battle is joined "on a wide field" at Karbanit. The Egyptians are defeated. The Pharaoh, who did not take part in the fighting, flees from Memphis to Thebes. The Assyrians pursue the retreating enemy and take Thebes[32]. The Egyptian navy, which is anchored at Thebes, is captured. Taharqa escapes to Nubia (Kush). The Assyrians advance to the Nubian border and then call off the pursuit. After the Assyrian troops have left, nobles ruling Egyptian nomes attempt to renew connections with the Pharaoh. The local Assyrian governors get wind of these attempts by intercepting messages. Several nobles are arrested and questioned. Prince Necho of Sais is deposed by the Assyrians as a consequence. Several cities, among them Tanis, Sais and Mendes continue the revolt, which however is easily crushed

---

32 According to the sources, the Assyrians refrain from sacking Thebes at this stage. Only in the campaign of 663/662 BC do they plunder the part of the city situated on the eastern bank of the Nile. The necropolis on the western bank is spared.

by locally-based Assyrian forces. The victors decide to set a gruesome example: the inhabitants of the rebellious towns are massacred, the survivors impaled and flayed. The skins are hung from the city walls. In view of this awful retaliation it is all the more surprising that Necho, who together with other rebellious governors had been brought before Ashurbanipal in chains, is spared. For whatever reasons, the king reinstates him as governor of Sais and Memphis. Ashurbanipal probably realizes that it is impossible to control a country as vast and distant as Egypt without at least a small number of reliable local allies. Other captives are not so lucky – they are executed at the king's orders. Necho's son Psammetichus will later liberate Egypt from Assyrian rule and once more unite the country under his rule – for now however he is a loyal ally of the Assyrian Great King in his struggle against the Nubian pharaohs. In the year 665 BC Ashurbanipal relates several incursions by mounted nomads that ravage the country "like locusts". The raiders turn out to be Cimmerians under their leader Dugdamme. The Cimmerians, coming from the southern Russian steppes via the Caucasus, threaten Assyria's northern neighbours, among them Urartu. Lydian king Gyges asks for Assyrian military assistance, but is denied. In 660 BC, the Lydians manage to repulse the Cimmerians without Assyrian support. Gyges sends Cimmerian prisoners to Ashurbanipal accompanied by envoys with the aim of forging an alliance, but Ashurbanipal again rejects the offer. Lydia is beyond the Assyrian sphere of interest. Assyrian rejection obliges Gyges to seek help elsewhere. He turns his diplomacy towards a resurgent Egypt. After his death in 644 BC his son and successor Ardys II again seeks support from the Assyrians, but the Assyrian response is not recorded. Cimmerian prince Dudamme is killed in battle in Cilicia in 642 BC. His son Sandak-kurru continues to raid Assyria and its neighbours.

❏ 665 BC: First campaign against Elam under its ruler Urtagu (Urtaki), who has invaded Babylonia. He is driven back into Elam, dying shortly after. He is succeeded by his cousin Te-Umman (Teumann or Teumman), a political upstart who is immediately involved in internal struggles, forcing him to dispose of political rivals. Two rightful heirs (Humban-Haltaš II and Urtagu II) are evacuated to Assyria with their families under cover of "a large retinue of archers". Ashurbanipal grants them political asylum and refuses to extradite them to Urartu at the new king's request. This causes new political tension as Elamite renegades wage war on the usurper.

❏ 664 BC: Assyrians campaign against Aramean king Bel-iqiša (Bel-iqisha) of the Gambulu tribe, whose home region lies between the city of Ur and the Ker-

cha River (Unku). Kushite Egyptian Pharaoh Taharqa dies. His nephew Tanotamun succeeds him to the throne and immediately embarks on reconquest of Egypt. This is partly successful.

❏ 663/662 BC: An Assyrian army invades Egypt and reconquers the territory lost in the previous year. They pursue Tanotamun, who has fled south from Memphis, and again take Thebes. Assyrian forces even venture into Nubia before returning home richly laden with the spoils of war. The campaign marks the end of the Ethiopian dynasty on the throne of the pharaohs.

❏ 660/659 BC: Assyrians campaign against Mannaean king Ahseri. The Mannaean capital fortress of Izirtu (Istati) is taken and the surrounding countryside pillaged by Assyrian troops. The Mannaeans rise against Ahseri, deposing and killing the hapless monarch. He is succeeded by his son Ualli, who seems to have been instrumental in his father's fall. Ashurbanipal, whose cavalry relies on a steady supply of Mannaean horses, recognizes Ualli as his father's legitimate heir. Ualli is required to deliver up an extra 30 horses in return for Ashurbanipal's support. He complies.

❏ 658–655 BC: With Lydian, Carian and Ionian support, Egyptians under Pharaoh Psammetichus I of the Saites dynasty expel Assyrians from Egypt. This event marks the end of the Assyrian Empire's apogee. Due to prolonged campaigns against Elam and Babylon and their allies Assyrians are unable to retaliate. Pressure from Scythians and Cimmerians on the northern frontier increases.

❏ 656–655 BC: Second campaign of Ashurbanipal against Elamite king Te-Umman, who has invaded northern Babylonia. An Assyrian army headed by a *turtānu* moves to intercept the invaders. Assyrians capture Elamite frontier fortress of Dur-ilu and advance into Elamite territory. Te-Umman is forced to take up a defensive position at the Ulai river near his capital, Susa. Assyrians cross the Ulai at Dullis and assault the Elamite positions. The battle at the Ulai River ends with a resounding Assyrian victory. Elamite losses are so huge that the slain are said to have choked the flow of the Ulai for three days. Te-Umman is wounded by an arrow and taken prisoner. He is beheaded shortly afterwards. His head is sent to Nineveh, where Ashurbanipal orders it to be hung from a tree in his garden. This gory example of Assyrian horticulture is depicted on an relief now at the British Museum. Itumi, the commanding general of the defeated Elamites, commits suicide. Several Elamite cities are besieged and captured. Ashurbanipal decides to divide the conquered Elamite territory

Fighting in the mountains

Austen Henry Layard, *The Monuments of Nineveh*, plate 70 (page 99), Digital library,
University of Heidelberg.

The relief shows Assyrian spearmen equipped with shields advancing in mountainous terrain. They are supported by archers. Captives and heads of slain enemies are being taken downhill for inspection. In order to maintain their foothold, several Assyrian soldiers are holding onto the branches of trees. Like the Assyrians, the enemies fighting downhill have formed groups of archers supported by shield bearers. The hemispherical cavity of the shields is worthy of note.

Assyrians destroy a plantation and slaughter livestock

Austen Henry Layard, *The Monuments of Nineveh*, plate 76 (page 105),
Digital library, University of Heidelberg.
Assyrian kings frequently refer to the destruction of economic and agricultural resources in enemy territory
unsuitable for occupation.

and instates Humban-nikash II (Ummanigaš), son of Urtak (Urtagu), as king in the area surrounding the cities of Susa and Madaktu. He gives Chidalu to prince Tammaritu[33]. This is a wise move designed to thwart Elamite aggression – Ashurbanipal chooses to adhere to the principle of "divide and conquer".

❑ 655 BC: Returning from the Elamite campaign, the Assyrian army does some mopping up, occupying Gambulu[34], territory on the Elamite and Babylonian border. Several small states have sprung up in the area, mostly inhabited by Arameans and Chaldeans. The Gambuleans under their king Dunanu are allied to the Elamites. Fighting deteriorates into a vicious guerilla war in the surrounding swamps and marshes, which is documented on Assyrian bas-reliefs at Nineveh. The capture of the Gambulean capital Sapibel (Shapi-bel) culminates in yet another bout of atrocities which Ashurbanipal chose to record for posterity despite (or because of) the fact that he was not present to witness them: "...the people I slaughtered like lambs." The survivors are deported. The unfortunate Dunanu is captured and cruelly tortured to death. Although it was normal for Assyrian kings to take the credit even for their subordinates' success, Ashurbanipal does in this instance appreciate his generals' feats. Other local rulers such as Umbakidinnu of Hidali and several Elamite princes see that all is lost and surrender.

❑ 654 BC: An embassy from Urartean king Rusas II pays a state visit to Nineveh. Relationships between Assyria and Urartu are cordial and the status quo is carefully observed. This is important in order to keep Assyria's northern frontier safe. Urartu needs its resources to hold Scythian and Cimmerian nomads at bay.

❑ 652–648 BC: "War between the Brothers": Ashurbanipal's younger brother Shamash-shum-ukin, King of Babylon, allies himself with Aramean and Chaldean tribes, among them the people of Bit Yakin, the Elamites, the Akkadians, and Arabs. Egypt supports the alliance after Elamites mobilise their forces in 653 BC.

❑ 648 BC: After four years of fighting, Ashurbanipal finally defeats the Babylonians and their allies. Sippar, Borsippa, Kutha and Babylon are placed under siege. Some of the besieged cities are infested with plague, which further undermines Babylonian resistance. Shamash-shum-ukin perishes in his burning palace as Assyrian troops breach the walls of Babylon. The vic-

tors exact a brutal revenge on Shamash-shum-ukin's retinue and the surviving population. At the same time, Assyrian forces are engaged in heavy fighting against the Babylonians' Elamite allies.

❑ 652 BC: Assyrians under Ashurbanipal inflict heavy defeat on Elamites under King Ummanigash II, an ally of Babylonia. Ummanigash is assassinated together with his family in 651 BC by his rival Tammaritu I, who seizes the Elamite throne. Like his predecessor, he is a sworn enemy of Ashurbanipal. Ironically, he is forced to yield his position to yet another contender for the throne, prince Indabibi, in 649 BC, and flees to Nineveh, where he receives political asylum. Ashurbanipal defeats Akkadian rebels and the Aramean and Chaldean tribes, and instates Assyrian governors in their territories. Indabibi (Atta-hamiti-Inshushinak) is defeated in 648 BC by future Elamite king Ummanaldash III. However, Ummanaldash may actually also have been Indabibi's son, and succeeded his father in orderly manner. According to the sources Atta-hamiti-Inshushinak died peacefully that same year. In 647 BC a usurper named Umbahabua seems to have seized the throne, but his reign is short-lived.

❑ 652/651 BC: Assyrians campaign against Arabs.

❑ 646–645 BC: Hostilities against Elam are renewed. Assyrians invade Elam and reconquer the former frontier fortress of Bit Imbi. Ummanaldash III escapes to the mountains. Ashurbanipal conquers the area around Madaktu and several other towns. Assyrians reinstate Tammaritu on the throne of Elam. He rises against Assyria but is defeated and brought back to Nineveh.

❑ 642–639 BC: Assyrians campaign against Elamites, this time under their king Ummanaldash III, who has again seized power. An Assyrian army again invades Elam, forcing Ummanaldash to again take to the mountains in the face of Assyrian superior numbers. Elamites retreat to Mount Saladri, where they are defeated and finally surrender. Ummanaldash is taken prisoner by his own entourage and handed over to the Assyrians. Elam, completely exhausted, is reduced to a small Assyrian province. The Elamite army is described in detail by Assyrian sources: they tell of captured archers, shield bearers, charioteers, horsemen and mounted archers. This points to a certain amount of similarities between the Elamite and Assyrian forces.

❑ 640–638 BC: The Assyrians army hits back hard against repeated Arab incursions under their king Uarte, an ally of Elam and Babylonia. Due to Assyrian campaigns against Elam this campaign is carried out

---

33   According to the sources Te-Umman had a son named Tamritu who was killed at the Ulai River. The similarity between the names is probably coincidental; nevertheless, a certain Tammaritu was to play a vital part in coming events.

34   The exact location of Gambulu is as yet unclear.

by a separate Assyrian force. After beating back the Arab invaders, who have been pillaging the Assyrian heartland, the Assyrians mount a counteroffensive and put numerous Arab settlements to the torch. Hoping for mercy, Uate travels to Nineveh and surrenders. He is locked in a dungeon together with a pack of dogs for his pains, and put on public display in a cage. Other Arab warbands that have ventured as far as Syria are annihilated piecemeal in several engagements.

❒ 639/638 BC: Urartean king Sarduri III sends envoys to Nineveh. His kingdom is under threat from Scythian raiders who have defeated the Cimmerians. These have returned to their original hunting grounds in the steppes around the Black Sea, where they will eventually be absorbed and assimilated by the Scythians, to vanish forever from the historical record. Hardly a trace remains of their existence today. Assyrian sources do not depict them owing to the scarcity of hostilities between the two peoples; other pictorial and written sources about these nomads of the steppes are rare and unreliable.

❒ 639–637 BC: Assyrians campaign against rebellious Phoenician city states. These are defeated together with their Arab Qedarite allies. Ammuladi, the new Arab king, is taken prisoner and put on display in a cage together with the wife of the hapless Uate. Ashurbanipal instates prince Abiate as the new Arab ruler. Abiate proves ungrateful by allying himself with the Nabataeans and rising against Assyrian political dominance. The Assyrians beat the allies at battle of Hurarina, winning large amounts of booty. Many Qedarites including the royal family are captured. The Assyrians are able to swiftly defeat the rebels by occupying vital oases, forcing the Arabs to drink the blood of their camels. The rebels are further decimated by disease. The amount of livestock captured is so plentiful that the price of a camel sinks to a mere half shekel of silver. After the Arabian tribes to the south have been subdued, the Assyrians turn their attention to the Phoenicians. Ushu and Akkon are captured and the populations deported. A last stand by Arabs and Phoenicians is brushed aside, the rebel generals are captured and flayed.

❒ 627 BC: Presumed year of Ashurbanipal's death. It is unclear whether he had resigned in 631 BC, and whether he already passed away in that year.

Decline and fall

In 626 BC the Chaldean Nabopolassar (Nabû-apla-uşur), general of the Assyrian army, becomes King of Babylon. Betraying his master Ashurbanipal, he sets about organizing Babylon's resurgence to its former glory. Ashurbanipal's successors, his son Ashur-etil-ilani, followed by Ashurbanipal's brother or general Sin-shar-ishkun, are unable to prevent this despite alliances with Egyptian pharaohs Psammetichus I and Necho II.

Babylon soon feels strong enough to wage outright war against a tottering Assyria. The Medes throw in their lot with the Babylonians and under their king Cyaxares II take the city of Ashur in 614 BC. Two years later the Medes capture Nineveh, the unfortunate Shin-shar-ishkun dying in the flames.

He is succeeded by Ashur-uballit II (Aššur-uballit), a former Assyrian *turtānu* who leads the remaining Assyrian forces to Harran and proclaims himself the new Assyrian king. The Medes have meanwhile defeated the Scythians and forced them into an alliance. They now join forces with the Babylonians and lay siege to Harran. An Egyptian relief force succeeds in evacuating the remnants of the Assyrian army, and the city finally falls in 610 BC. Ashur-uballit II's attempt to recapture the city fails.

Pharaoh Necho II reinforces his army and marches north to contain rising Babylonian power in the region and to secure Egyptian influence in Palestine. The Egyptians defeat the Babylonians' Judean allies under King Josiah at Megiddo in 607 BC, but they are incapable of stemming the tide of Assyrian decline. The fate of Ashur-uballit II remains unknown. So loathsome was the Assyrians' name among their former subjects that nearly all Assyrian cities are reduced to rubble in the ensuing campaigns.

In a final battle for mastery of the Middle East and what is left of the once proud Assyrian Empire, the Babylonians defeat an Egyptian army under Necho II, which has ventured into Syria. The Babylonians are led by Nabopolassar's son and successor Nebuchadnezzar II (Nabū-kudurrī-ušur). The Egyptian army is reinforced by Assyrian contingents, but these are again defeated at Hama together with their Egyptian allies. This engagement marks the ultimate conclusion to the story of Assyrian power in the Middle East. The Egyptians withdraw from Syria and Palestine, thus putting an end to all hopes of restoring Assyria as a political entity in the region.

THE ASSYRIAN ARMY

Composition

Sources regarding the Assyrian army are scanty. Many aspects of Assyrian military organisation and administration remain completely unknown or conjectural at best. In other words, our knowledge regarding topics as various as recruitment, training, medical care, burial rites, military justice, decorations, careers, morale, duty rosters, hierarchies and ranks, pay, rewards, booty distribution, leisure, pensions, intelligence, military administration, transmission of orders and lines of communication is extremely patchy. These shortcomings notwithstanding, the sheer size of the Assyrian Empire and our knowledge of political events do allow us to conclude that the degree and standards of Neo-Assyrian military organisation must have been truly remarkable.

The root of all Assyrian military success was a well-equipped army of professional soldiers[35] composed of both Assyrians and other ethnicities, a militia, and the auxiliary contingents provided by vassals and allies. King Tiglath-Pileser III undertook a number of reforms to improve the army's already well-established efficiency. He transformed the Assyrian forces into a standing army. Heretofore, the milita system had permitted the calling up of peasants only after the conclusion of the harvest in May. Campaigns were thus reduced to the span of time between harvest and sowing time, when the Assyrian peasant-soldier was forced to return to his farming. The expansion of the Empire no longer allowed for this kind of system (as the Romans were later likewise forced to recognise), calling for a standing force which could remain in the field for years on end if required. For example, the siege of the Syrian city of Arpad took no less than three years (742–739 BC). The loyalty of the troops was secured by regular pay and good conditions of service as well as a share in the booty after a successful campaign or siege. All supreme command rested in the hands of the royal family and high-ranking generals or viziers. Since the Great Kings claimed power from the gods, their authority remained virtually unchallenged.

If the situation became desperate even the Sargonids could resort to conscription. The obligation to serve in the militia formed part of Assyrian fiscal law and affected peasants, artisans, cities and their immediate surroundings, and owners of large estates. Especially the inhabitants of frontier provinces habitually found themselves actively containing enemy incursions until the the field army moved in to deal with the trouble. It was the duty of the provincial governor to keep the militia up to strength,

and a large proportion of Assyrian males owned arms, be it a bow or a pair of spears for hunting, or a simple sling or dagger. Arsenals provided for anyone lacking even this basic equipment. Defending their homes was in the population's own interest, and they were quite willing to do so until the king or his generals arrived to sort things out. Local contingents were quite capable of standing their ground until a larger force arrived.

Keeping a militia-based force in the field unfailingly resulted in economic recession, since the peasants and artisans-turned-soldiers were unable to work in their professions at home. Compensation was necessary and made available in the form of pay, tax benefits, and booty. The sources imply that free Assyrians, loyal vassals and even conscripts enjoyed social privileges and royal support, which ultimately ensured a fairly high standard of living judging by the standards of the time. This naturally created a high degree of loyalty towards the king himself, whose military success was also explained with the omnipotence and almighty power of Assyria's pantheon, which time and again proved itself superior to the gods of Ashur's enemies. Although they did not outright deny their existence, the Assyrians regularly removed the images of the deities of defeated nations from their temples. Setting this ostentative gesture of authority aside, they seem to have displayed a remarkable amount of religious tolerance. Occasionally religious statues and objects of religious veneration were even restored to their temples as a mark of benevolence. It is surely safe to say that Assyria's wars were not conducted out of any sort of religious fervour. Nevertheless, the conviction that his king was under protection of powerful gods must have been both comforting and reassuring to the simple Assyrian warrior. Sources with a military context mention the *sab šarri* (sab sharri), which roughly translates as "the king's men". The phrase referred to both levies and the *kišir šarruti* (kishir sharruti), the standing Assyrian royal army. It goes without saying that the professional soldiers of the *kišir šarruti* enjoyed a more thorough and regular training than the militia: specialists whose skills demanded regular and careful training such as the élite units of cavalry, charioteers and engineers were professional soldiers. This also applied to the core of the infantry, and the military musicians. Both militia and soldiers of the standing army underwent some form of basic training to ensure discipline, coherence and a certain tactical homogenity in the huge armies the Great King was capable of raising. Other parts of the army comprised artificers and the soldiers of the transport corps. The latter are probably the troops referred to as *hupšu* in one of Sargon II's commentaries, but in the context of sieges the word may also denote the pioneers and engineers in charge of the siege engines. Assyrian baggage trains mostly consisted of large caravans. The royal army

---

35 These military professionals, many of them mercenaries, might serve the King himself or one of his relatives, but high-ranking court officials, princes and provincial governors also kept private troops, which in case of war were placed under central command.

Various Assyrian troop types
Victor Place, *Ninive et l'Assyrie*, vol. 3, plate 61 (page 77).
Digital library, University of Heidelberg.

This beautifully executed illustration after a relief excavated at Nineveh depicts several Assyrian troops types. We may discern bow- and spear-armed cavalry, infantry spearmen equipped with shields, archers, and slingers. The men are equipped with various helmets and headdresses, lamellar cuirasses, and breastplates; the horses are decked with protective bardings either of leather or fabric.

was further accompanied by the Great King's bodyguard, numerous officials and courtiers, and the provincial governors.

It was important for a king or royal prince to secure the loyalty or at best even the devotion of his soldiers. It was the soldiers who supported Esarhaddon's bid for the throne against the determined resistance of his brothers in the wake of their father's assassination. Due to its geographic position Assyria was locked in a struggle with surrounding neighbours which lasted for centuries. This forced the army to constantly reassess its potential and develop its skills to encounter an ever-increasing number and variety of enemies. This development also resulted in a concentration of military know-how and equipment, which was provided by a constant flow of booty and tributes, but which was also acquired through trade and local production. Arsenals and storehouses were established in key cities.

Horses for the cavalry and the chariot arm were supplied by the nations to the north and east of Assyria as part of their tributes to the Great King. Especially the Medes and Manneans were excellent horse breeders, and their animals accordingly sought after by the military. Control of these regions and their human and equine inhabitants was thus a military necessity vital for the Empire's survival. The acquisition of horses was the responsibility of the *mušarkisu*, a group of officials in charge of remounts, and the maintenance, training and sustenance of cavalry mounts. They were immediately responsible to the Great King himself. The number of chariot and cavalry horses was carefully recorded twice a year, often in the king's presence.

On campaign, the Assyrian army consisted of several contingents. The Assyrian regular forces were supplemented by the auxiliary contingents supplied by allies, and by vassal kings and princes. The governors (*bēl pīḫati*) were respnsible for raising the militia, whose units were named after their native region. The army also recruited foreign auxiliaries and mercenaries from beyond the frontiers. There is evidence that Assyrian armies numbered Scythians, Ionians, Israelites, Syrians, Arameans and Chaldeans[36] in their ranks. Especially the warriors of the Aramean tribes fought both for Assyria and its enemies for centuries. They can be easily spotted on Assyrian reliefs due to their conspicuous appearance.

The majority of troops belonging to an Assyrian army were lightly equipped. For instance, the Arameans in the sources are armed with bows and make do without protective armour. Assyrian armies were a polyglot affair consisting of soldiers from a multitude of nations, all differently equipped and clothed. The Great King's bodyguard consisted of soldiers from eleven nations alone. Foreign auxiliaries were organized into *kiṣru* (cohorts). The sources mention *kiṣru* of Cimmerians, Philistines, citizens of Akko, and Elamite archers. Some auxiliaries depicted in pictorial sources may be Israelites or Arameans. Often defeated enemies found themselves recruited into the ranks of the Assyrian army. Any misgivings would have been tempered by the privileges of being a subject of the Great King and the privileges and rights this entailed. It will not have taken most of them long to realize that this was preferable to deportation and slavery. Thus the king hoped to win over former enemies and turn them into loyal and diligent soldiers.

The composition of the army

The Assyrian army consisted of
- Regular standing troops (royal household troops, forces garrisoning cities and fortresses).
- Local governors' (*bēl pīḫati*) regular troops, household troops of members of the royal family and high-ranking officials.
- Assyrian levies and provincial militia.
- Vassal troops.
- Allied contingents.
- Auxiliaries recruited for the duration of a campaign.

The proportion of infantry, cavalry and chariots could vary within individual contingents. Armament and equipment strongly depended on a unit's status, proficiency, and ethnic background. Auxiliary contingents rarely comprised chariots. Apart from horsemen, an auxiliary cavalry force might also include soldiers mounted on mules or camels (the latter were usually of Arab origin). Quality and amount of individual armament and equipment varied, and the line between light and heavy troops was fuzzy at best. A certain degree of uniformity and prevailing high-quality equipment may be presumed in the case of the king's élite guard units. These were organised according to their military duties and functions, and ranked among the regular standing troops. The forces manning the fortresses and the garrisons of the cities also formed part of the regular army.

---

36 Arameans who had permanently settled in Babylonian territory were called Chaldeans.

Sāb šarri: "The King's Men"

I. Kiṣir šarrūti (professional soldiers):
  I. 1 Regulars (city and fortress garrisons, arsenal guards)
  I. 2 Household troops:
  - Lifeguards *(ša šēpē)*[37], chariots, cavalry and infantry
  - Personal bodyguards and armed retainers (*ša qurbūte* and *mutēr pūti*. The latter seems to have been another type of lifeguard; the name only appears in the Neo-Assyrian period during Sennacherib's reign).[38]

II: Conscripts

The guardsmen and professional soldiers could be Assyrians or hail from a multitiude of other ethnic groups in the Assyrian empire. The conscripts served as soldiers, but also performed as craftsmen or baggage attendants; this service was part of their fiscal duties.

The standing army (kiṣir šarrūti), which could be commanded either by the king himself or a trusted and proven relative or official, could be assembled in a fairly short amount of time. A cumbersome call to arms and subsequent assembly of the entire army including provincial troops and auxiliaries on the other hand took time and could prove costly if enemy intelligence got wind of the size and objective of the Assyrian forces. The sources claim that some Assyrian campaigns were conducted so swiftly that only parts of the standing army, mostly household troops, actually took part. This hastily assembled force was able to surprise and overpower the enemy, who had clearly not reckoned with such a speedy appearance of the Assyrian force. The mobilisation of only a fraction of the army, even if they were crack household units, was risky however and only promising if conducted against an enemy who was expected to be caught off guard or who only had inferior troops at his disposal.

In 711 BC, Sargon II waged an Assyrian *blitzkrieg* against the renegade King Yamani of Ashdod, before the latter was able to assemble allied contingents. In his account of the campaign, Sargon himself reports that "...with anger in my heart I abstained from assembling the brunt of my troops and set up no camp. Together with my heroes, who did not leave my side even in times of peace, I marched on Ashdod."

In its heyday, the core of the Neo-Assyrian Empire comprised no less than 27 provinces. The fractioning of the empire into comparatively small provinces ensured that no governor grew too big for his boots.

When integrating foreign troops into the army, it was advisable to observe the ratio between these untried and potentially unreliable soldiers and the loyal and trustworthy veterans. In order to get a feel for the numbers involved when an Assyrian army took the field, it is worth noting that in the course of his campaigns Sargon II added 500 chariots along with their crews to his own forces, and several tens of thousands of archers and spear-armed infantry with shields[39][40]. These numbers derive from the very few sources which have come down to us. If one supposes that despite this massive boost of manpower the Assyrian contingents in the royal army still formed the majority of the troops to ensure the army's overall loyalty and discipline, a strong Assyrian army would have consisted of several thousands of chariots and horsemen, and several ten thousands of infantry. It is surely not implausible to assume that the Great King was effortlessly capable of raising an army of more than 50 000 men. Even Assyrian sources predating the Sargonids mention armies numbering 120 000 men; at the time, Assyrian armies still consisted mostly of levies alone.

---

39 Very often the spearmen used their shields to protect the archers from enemy missiles. This was practised in all arms of the Assyrian army, infantry, cavalry and chariots, and may well have been a genuine Assyrian tactical innovation.

40 Obviously these figures ought to be treated with a certain amount of caution, as Assyrian sources tend to exaggerate; nevertheless, they do give us a certain idea of the sheer mass of troops the Assyrians managed to integrate into their own armies.

---

37 One of Sargon II's élite units consisted of 1 000 horse.

38 Personal bodyguards did not merely serve as security forces but also took a variety of other responsibilities. Evidently they were confidantes of the king holding officer ranks.

Royal household troops

Lightly armed warriors lacking helmets (and quite often even body armour) are frequently depicted among the retinue of Assyrian rulers. They appear particularly often in the reliefs at Khorsabad (Dur Šarrukin) describing the events during the campaigns of Sargon II. Apart from regular armament consisting of swords, bows and spears, these soldiers also carry maces or canes, evidently as a sign of élite status. The troop types concerned can be classified as archers and infantry equipped with spears and shields. In his report on the campaign of 714 BC, Sargon II mentions "horses walking by [his] side". This is possibly a reference to his personal bodyguards, who were frequently also employed on special missions.

The plate shows several of these troops in the aftermath of battle. An Assyrian royal bodyguard could expect to see a reasonable amount of action – King Sargon II himself was surprised and killed in an ambush sprung by enemy forces. A diadem or headband seems to have formed the characterisitc headdress of these soldiers. The main weapon of the horse guards shown in the plate was the bow. The weapon was stored in a leather bowcase along with the arrows. As a protection against rain, the bowcase featured a leather cover. Especially the powerful composite bows, whose parts were glued together in a time-consuming and complicated process, were prone to disintegrating under damp conditions. The horse wears a chamfrom and a peytral combining protective and decorative elements. Both peytrals and chamfroms have been found chiefly in Urartean contexts, but Assyrian reliefs also attest to their use in the Assyrian army. Both pieces of horse equipment could be adorned with religious imagery.

Apart from the personal bodyguards described above, the *ša šēpē* also performed lifeguard functions. In contrast to their comrades in the *ša qurbūte*, they were more heavily equipped and armed. Apart from the lightly armed personal bodyguards, Assyrian sources also depict armoured troops wearing cuirasses and helmets as part of the royal retinue. It appears obvious that there was a need for more heavily equipped troops which were capable of meeting appropriately a threat which could not be contained by merely a handful of personal guards. The warrior in the right background wears lamellar armour. The warrior in the left background caries a shield and is a member of the foot guards. Legwear and shoes varied according to climatic conditions and the soldier's military function. Horsemen were already equipped with breeches and laced boots.

It goes without saying that regarding numbers the sources are not to be taken at face value. When Shalmaneser III went to war against twelve allied kings, whose forces included Syrians, Hittites, Israelites and Arabs, he gives the following enemy strengths present at the battle of Qarqar in 853 BC:

> 1 200 chariots, 1 200 horses, 20 000 soldiers of Hadadidri,
> 700 chariots, 700 cavalry mounts, 10 000 soldiers of Irhuleni of Hamath,
> 2 000 chariots, 10 000 soldiers of Ahabbu[41],
> 500 soldiers from Que (Cilicia),
> 1 000 soldiers from Muŝki (Anti-aurus mountains)
> 10 chariots and 10 000 soldiers from Arqa (city near Tripolis)
> 200 soldiers of Matinubali of Arwad,
> 200 soldiers from Ushu,
> 30 chariots and 10 000 soldiers of Adunubali (Adunnu Baal) of Shianu/Siyannu,
> 1 000 camels[42] of Gindibu the Arab,
> 100[43] soldiers of Ba'asa the Aramean.

Several Assyrian sources on the battle survive, with considerably diverging figures. For instance, the enemy losses given by these documents vary between 14 000 and 25 000. If we assume that each chariot was manned by two soldiers only, then the enemy army must have numbered around 70 000, rendering losses totalling 14 000 a realistic quantity. This would however also mean that the Assyrian force must have totalled at least the same number of soldiers.

It is interesting to examine the composition of the individual contingents involved in this example. The enemy infantry outnumbered the amount of enemy chariots, which totalled 3 900 (this is rather doubtful). The cavalry consisted of 1900 horsemen. Whether the other contingents, whose troop types are not distinctly defined, contained contingents of cavalry remains impossible to tell. Sargon II gives an account of the incorporation of chariots of defeated enemies into his own army.

In his third campaign against the Syrian princes in 846 BC, Shalmaneser III claims to have fielded a force of 120 000 soldiers: "In the fourteenth year of my reign I raised the levy far and wide, and with 120 000 troops I crossed the swollen Euphrates". The reference to the levy seems to imply the employment of mercenaries instead of regulars. Smaller forces could be dispatched if the situation al-lowed. In 750 BC the Assyrian provincial governor of Suhi sent 105 chariots, 200 horse, and 3 000 infantry to deal with an incursion of 2 000 Aramean tribesmen into his territory.

Cuneiform inscriptions from the time of Sargon II can indirectly provide an idea of the composition of an Assyrian army which fought against Prince Muttalu of Kummuh in 708 BC. Sargon II ordered a *turtānu* to pursue the defeated enemy force, placing 150 chariots, 1 500 horse, 20 000 bowmen and 10 000 shieldbearers under his command.

The sheer size of the Assyrian Empire with its large number of provinces guaranteed fairly stable and impressive military strength, the complete mobilisation of which was a lengthy affair, and restrictions were imposed by the logistical possibilities of the time. Even in times of emergency, the Assyrians were careful not to completely deplete the border provinces of troops since this would literally have invited enemy raids.

Assyrian cavalry regiments were named after cities. There were Assur, Arrapha, Arzuhina and Erbil regiments. One squadron, which is impossible to place accurately, was raised from deported men. A Babylonian-Aramean and a Samaritan cavalry regiment were both formed under Tiglath-Pileser III.

The proficiency of Assyrian military administration guaranteed swift and numerous recruitment of units. The authorities oversaw the recruiting, training and provisioning of the troops, and the complex logistics this involved. Arsenals, storehouses and granaries were built. In this context, the punctual delivery of tributes from vassal rulers, allies and defeated enemies was absolutely vital, since these goods were indispensable for the sustenance of the armies in the field.

The reign of the Sargonids marked the highpoint of Assyrian military and political power. Many foreign soldiers were compelled to serve the Great Kings, and the reliefs from this time depict a rich variety of warriors from numerous ethnic backgrounds. Many however chose to serve of their own accord. Decent terms and conditions of service, for instance a fair and generous distribution of booty and reliable and plentiful supplies, kept mercenaries serving in the Assyrian army plentiful and happy. Newly recruited mercenaries were equipped from the royal arsenals at the king's expense until they acquired the means to equip themselves out of their own pockets. The largest contingent of mercenaries consisted of soldiers recruited among the Aramean tribes.

Standards in the Assyrian army were high, and recruits were trained accordingly. For example, the cooperation between archers and shield-bearers had to run smoothly if Assyrian strategy was to prove efficient; teamwork and tactical interaction were therefore extremely important. It was the heavily-armed infantryman's job to to shield the archer assigned to him from enemy missiles, be he on foot, mounted, or part of a chariot crew. Deployment had to be swift, flexible and precise, as did advance and

---

41   This is the biblical King Ahab of Israel. It remains highly doubtful if he was capable of providing 2 000 chariots. The figure is probably a scribe's error.

42   The word "camel" must be interpreted as "dromedary", which serves as a riding animal in desert regions to this day.

43   Probably the number ought to read 1 000; the source is impossible to interpret clearly. Again, possibly a scribe's mistake, or an omission.

retreat and the interaction between the different troop types in battle, for example between the cavalry and the chariots. All this required careful and frequent training.

Meticulous planning and staff work was a prerequisite of Assyrian military prowess. The Assyrian army relied on an experienced and well-trained officer corps with a clear-cut hierarchy, standardized orders and military signalling. A well-equipped corps of engineers was responsible for the construction of camps and siegeworks as well as the bridging of rivers, often in the presence of the enemy. Assyrian reliefs show numerous siege engines, whose construction, operation and maintenance required considerable technological know-how and scientific expertise. Logistics and transport were another area vital to Assyrian military success.

Assyrians were rarely beaten. What did it take, then, to defeat such a proud and efficient military organism? An enemy force only stood a chance of defeating an Assyrian army if it was well-equipped and more numerous. Enemy leaders acknowledged Assyrian military excellence by creating alliances which often forced the Assyrians to compete with overwhelming numbers on several fronts. The choice of topographically suitable terrain to contain the destructive force of the Assyrian cavalry and chariots was also important. Agile and swift-moving forces such as the Cimmerians and Scythians could gain a vital edge over a more cumbersome Assyrian army. The Sargonids' military dominance of the Middle East remained largely unchallenged if one discounts the Egyptians, the Urarteans, the Elamites, the Medes and, later, the Neo-Babylonian armies which alone were capable of posing a serious challenge to Assyrian forces. Detailed accounts of battles and sieges remain as yet undiscovered. It is a great pity that Assyria's enemies remain largely silent. Of course Assyrian sources habitually ignore or gloss over military reverses so that we can only say very little about Assyrian defeats and setbacks, and why they occurred.

Branches of service

The three main troop types of which the Assyrian army consisted were infantry *(zukū)*, cavalry *(pēṭḫal)*, and chariots. These were supplemented by engineers and transport troops. All of these were subdivided into categories charged with separate duties. For example, cuneiform inscriptions define specific cavalry units designated for reconnaissance and despatch bearing duties. The soldiers' main weapons were the bow, the throwing spear and the lance; to this the infantry added the sling.

The smallest tactical unit was the group of ten commanded by a *rab ešerte*[44], a rank roughly equivalent to a modern lance corporal or minor NCO. Five such groups formed a unit of 50 commanded by a *rab ḫanšî*, a captain. Several of these units formed a cohort *(kišru)*, which was led by an officer holding the rank of a *rab kišir*. These unit names applied to the entire Assyrian army.

Research on other Middle Eastern armies of the period has shown that some armies were organized into units of 50, 100, 500 and 1 000 men. Such standardization would probably have existed only in the regular Assyrian forces while it appears improbable with allies, vassal troops and auxiliaries. Just how strong a regular *kišru* actually was, remains mostly conjecture.

Sub-units contained soldiers armed with a variety of weapons, but units composed solely of archers or spearmen also existed. Apart from his main weapons, a soldier's individual armament could also include a sword, dagger, knife, or hatchet. Apart from their weapons, soldiers were equipped with body armour such as helmets, corselets, chest protectors, shields and broad studded belts. Underneath his armour, the soldier wore a tunic. Footwear consisted either of sandals or laced boots, some men went barefoot. In fact ethnic origin and status (e. g. conscript or mercenary) seems to have played a certain role as to how a soldier dressed and equipped himself.

Since equipment consisted of a wide range of materials varying in form, colour and appearance, an Assyrian army must have offered a fairly colourful, occasionally even hotch-potch appearance. For example, one relief shows Assyrian soldiers wearing no less than seven types of helmet. Since only a few reliefs were originally painted and the colours of those that were have almost completely faded, we are mostly ignoriant as to how and which materials (e. g. iron, leather, bronze) were combined in a soldier's individual panoply.

Reliefs commemorating pivotal events such as the surrender of Lachish or the submission of the Elamites following their defeat on the River Ulai show well-equipped warriors with a comparatively uniform appearance surrounding the king. These could be guardsmen, and possibly the sculptors here wished to idealize Assyrian military appearance and equipment. A second glance reveals that

---

44 The word *rab* denotes a leader, while *ešerte* stands for the figure 10, the rank thus signifies "leader [of] ten".

Plate 29. Triumph of the

an King. (Kouyunjik.)

Assyrian commander wearing helmet

Austen Henry Layard, *A Second Series of Monuments of Nineveh*, plate 29 (page 43).
Digital library, University of Heidelberg.

Assyrian kings are often depicted wearing the *tiara*. Evidently the artist wished to point out the king's person to the viewer. Nevertheless, if the military situation required, e. g. in battle, Assyrian kings were not above donning helmets and body armoir. The above relief was discovered in Sennacherib's South-Western Palace at Kuyunjik in Nineveh. Layard identifies the general mounted on his chariot as King Sennacherib.

even these warriors are not uniformly equipped however, and that small differences exist in the shape of helmets and the size and forms of the scales forming the soldiers' cuirasses. We may thus deduce that even among the élite household troops equipment was never completely standardized, which considering the manufacturing methods of the age would have been quite impossible at any rate.

A specific number of cavalry, infantry and chariot *kiṣru* formed an army's core. Since no coherent Assyrian source providing information about tactics and deployments has survived, we can only suppose that these units were deployed in a certain coherent order both on the march and in battle. It is obvious that a military machine as efficient as the Assyrian army would have had fixed structures to put its power into a maximum amount of effect. Two so-called royal highways, along which a string of post stations was maintained, existed to facilitate communication and a speedy movement of troops. Night marches were common.

Leadership and command

Supreme commander of the Assyrian army was the Great King himself, although he not always chose or was able to command the entire army in person. Often the army was divided into several corps operating in different theatres of war at the same time. These contingents would would either be commanded by the royal princes or high-ranking officers or court officials, as was the case during Sennacherib's campaign against Judah in 701 BC. One force under the king himself laid siege to Lachish while a detached force under the command of a *turtānu*, the *rab ša rēšē* (chief eunuch), and the *rab šāqê* (chief cup bearer) besieged Jerusalem. During the reign of King Esarhaddon, whose health was notoriously poor and who had the misfortune of dying while on campaign, armies were frequently commanded by a *turtānu* (field marshal). Esarhaddon's son and successor Ashurbanipal also often left the command of his armies to his generals. In a letter to his father Sargon II, Ashurbanipal lists the most important Assyrian dignitaries, who commonly also held military commands or performed logistical and administrative duties. Below the king, the queen and the crown prince ranked:

- The chamberlain or vizier *(sukallu)*,
- The field marshal *(turtānu)*,
- The chief justice *(sartennu)*,
- The treasurer *(masennu)*, and the vice chamberlain.

Other sources also mention
- The royal herald *(nāgir ekalli)*,
- The chief cup bearer *(rab šāqê)*,
- The chief eunuch *(rab ša rēšē)*,
- The steward *(rab bēti)*.

It is unclear whether one of these offices is identical with that of the vice-chamberlain. To the holders of these elevated positions must be added the provincial governors and their administrative and military staffs, and a small number of nobles. The prefects *(šaknu)* were probably mostly charged with military administration. A *turtānu* was frequently supported by a *chanu*, but we do not know whether this was a high military rank or simply a kind of adjutant. The high-ranking court officials would assume military commands in times of war, thus forming not just a civilian but also a military social élite. This custom ensured close cooperation with the king at all times, but it was vital for these men to possess not only administrative but also military skills. The *rab šāqê* is frequently mentioned by the sources as a leader of armies or detachments. It is tempting to assume that the royal cup bearer was actually the commander of all troops directly assigned to the king and the royal princes. King Esarhaddon despatched his trusted *rab šāqê* Šanubušû with a small army to bring to heel the rebellious town of Amul. Since it was custom to seek divine protection and advice before a military campaign or far-reaching political decisions, Esarhaddon's enquired to the sun god Shamash about the campaign's chances of success. His plea to the sun god was recorded for posterity and has survived.

Other high-ranking officers in the Assyrian army were the *rab mūgi* of chariots and the cavalry, also referred to in some sources as *muarkisu*. Either these officers were merely the commanders of the army's two respective branches, or they might also have served as the *turtānu's* deputies.

In spite of a further handful of surviving Assyrian rank names, e. g. *šalšu kiššati* (commander of three units), *rab kašzi* (commander of archers), and *amelša bitḫallē* (officer of horse), the rank order and command structure of the Neo-Assyrian army remain mostly unclear. As mentioned above, military commanders were also expected to perform other duties besides commanding the forces entrusted to them – Esarhaddon sent his *rab mūgi* Nabusarusur (Nâbû-šar-uṣūr) on a diplomatic mission to prince Ikkalu of Muški in the city of Aruada to check upon the latter's loyalty[45]. Nabusarusur seems to have been both reliable and able, since Ashurbanipal made him his

---

45   This is also mentioned in Esarhaddon's enquiry to Shamash.

rab šāqê and entrusted him with the command of the Assyrian force designated to reconquer a number of fortresses which had been captured by the Manneans – or to restore them to Assyrian control by means of negotiation. Later Nabusarusur led a campaign against the Gambuleans and Urbi.

Since chariots and cavalry partly operated in separate groups on both wings, Assyrian command structure must have catered for this complex tactical circumstance. Officers would also have been assisted by deputies to take over in case of injury, disease, or death. The Assyrian army frequently marched in separate columns and divisions, so we may conclude that these forces required separate commands and staffs.

There were at least two different turtānu during Esarhaddon's reign, since wars were frequently fought in different regions at the same time. Scholars suggest that a turtānu was responsible for the military maintenance and defence of a certain area within the empire which was assigned to his command. Possibly there existed an administrative and strategic north-south divide. Sometimes forces were mobilised according to their respective distance from the proposed theatre of operations. For example, for Ashurbanipal's Egyptian campaign the Assyrian forces based west of the Euphrates were mobilised first. These were placed under a turtānu's command. After that the *rab šāqê* himself took the field with the forces of the king and the governors from the other side of the river.

The level of Assyrian command structure between the generals and the *rab kišir* cohort commander remains obscure[46]. Possibly experienced and reliable cohort commanders were given command of several cohorts at once. Armies were accompanied by priests whose duty it was to perform the sacred rites, prayers and sacrifices necessary to secure divine favour and thus victory.

From the scant information yielded by various sources we may reconstruct the following conjectural rank and command structure:

Commander-in-chief (the Great King, a royal prince, a *turtānu*, the *rab šāqê* (chief cup bearer), or *rab ša rēšē* (chief eunuch).

Sartemu (chief justice), *sukallu* (vizier), *masennu* (treasurer), *nāgir ekalli* (palace herold); all of the latter probably formed a kind of general staff.

Chanu (military adjutants of the general staff; experienced and reliable palace officials and courtiers)

Rab mūgi (commanders of the various arms of service[47])

Rab kišir (cohort commander)

Rab ḫanšî (captain of a company of 50 soldiers)

Rab ešerte (10-man section commander)

It is possible that the cavalry, infantry and chariot sections of different divisions were assigned to various *rab mūgi* responsible to the respective *turtānu* or *rab ša rēšē*. Infantry, cavalry, chariots, engineers, and the majority of auxiliaries [48]were organized into cohorts commanded by *rab mūgi*. If guard or royal household units were dispatched to serve with divisions other than the king's, these also seem to have been organized into cohorts. Thus the cohort system applied to all branches of the Assyrian armed forces irrespective of rank (infantry, cavalry and engineers, for chariots see below), from tribal levies to the troops of the royal household. We do not know just how large a cohort was, and how many platoons and companies exactly they were composed of. Unit strength probably depended on the number of men available, and how many troops the situation at hand required. The chariots were organized into groups of 50. Each of these units was commanded by a *rab ḫanšî*.

Certain Assyrian military functions and ranks defy satisfactory identification. For instance, *rab pēthal* means "commander of cavalry", but the specific function of this rank remains unclear if one takes into account the wide range of responsibilities and functions a commander can have in a modern context. Prefects *(šaknu)* and recruiting officers *(mušarkisu)* seem to have existed in all arms of service, the latter also being responsible for the acquisition of cavalry remounts. There were also officers holding the rank of *rab kallabri*, a rank comparable to adjutant. These lightly armed soldiers were also employed as despatch riders and messengers.

Peculiar to the chariots and cavalry was the rank of *rab urâte*; these officers commanded units differing in size from the conventional section, company or cohort. These units could be smaller or larger than cohort-size, for example the royal horse guards, the guard and household

---

46   The Egyptian army also was organized into units of 50 men, which proves that armies of the time were similarly organized. This circumstance probably also affected tactics.

47   Since weknow that there was a *rab mūgi* respectively in charge of the chariots and the cavalry, we may assume that another of these officers commanded the infantry.

48   Sources mention cohort commanders of Cimmerian cavalry in Assyrian service in the years 780 to 763 BC.

Assyrian foot archer and infantry spearman

Reliefs frequently show a tactical symbiosis popular in the Assyrian army – foot and horse archers were covered by detached spearmen providing protection with their shields. If attacked, the spearman would employ his polearm to keep the enemy at a distance.

The archer wears a pointed helmet of bronze widely popular in both Assyrian and Urartean armies of the time. It is modelled on a surviving example formerly in the Axel Guttmann collection, Berlin. No cheekpieces survive, but not all helmets of this type seem to have possessed them. The helmet in question has holes around its lower rim to attach a lining. Two additional holes on each side may have served to fasten a chinstrap or cheekplates of organic material. The archer's secondary armament merely consists of a dagger. His corselet is composed of semicircular bronze scales.

The spearman carries a tall shield made of reeds and leather. The upper and lower rims are reinforced with leather, but concrete archaeological evidence for this is lacking. Other shields of this type were produced in a plywood manner using small strips of wood, and bound with metal. He wears a bipartite conical helmet, one half of the bowl made of bronze, the other of iron. Both halves were riveted together along a raised ridge running from front to back. This unique helmet find was also formerly part of the Guttmann collection. To what extent this peculiar manufacturing method added to the helmet's actual protective quality, or whether it was designed chiefly for show, remains anyone's guess. Again, the helmet possesses holes along the lower rim to accommodate a lining, and holes to attach either a chinstrap or cheekpieces. The foot soldier not only provides cover for his archer comrade, he has also slung his quiver over his shoulder. Though some quivers made completely of bronze have been found, most consisted of a combination of leather and bronze covering.

chariot squadrons, or provincial contingents. All of these units were probably ad hoc formations responding to the requirements of a specific military objective. Sources also mention "the commander of archers", but we do not know how strong the formation in question was.

At least the junior officers of the Assyrian army seem to have hailed from a variety of ethnic backgrounds. This was the natural result of the Assyrian custom of incorporating defeated enemies into their own army.

Tactics and control

In order to control an army in battle, a general must have at his disposal a certain range of tactics and the means to relay his orders to subordinate commanders. The tactical dispositions of the armies involved in the conflicts of this era must have been fairly similar since all consisted of the same elements of infantry, cavalry, and chariots. All of these arms were structured according to armament and tactical function. The infantry was composed of heavily-armed spearmen with shields, archers, and slingers. Other soldiers were armed with maces, clubs, axes, and hatchets. These were mostly secondary arms or were carried by specialist units[49]. Daggers were used as close-combat weapons. Many reliefs depict teams of archers and shield-bearing heavy infantry, the spearman's job being to protect the archer from enemy missiles. Both soldiers formed the minimal tactical unit within a kiṣru. However, there also seem to have existed kiṣru composed of only one type of armament. Reliefs depict units consisting solely of archers or heavy infantry. Again, this seems to have been a response to individual tactical requirements. Archers positioned at a certain distance from the enemy did not necessarily need protection from enemy missiles, and storming a fortified position or engaging enemy infantry was a job primarily for heavily armed troops trained to fight at close range.

Reliefs depicting larger groups of infantry frequently show archers and spearmen deployed in alternating ranks or files. As long as the spearman stood beside "his" archer, he was able to protect both himself and his comrade while the latter kept the enemy at a distance with his bow. If the order was given to advance or in the case of an all-out enemy attack, the lines of spearmen would either pass through the ranks of archers or advance their files and form a solid battle line ahead of the missile troops, who would then still be in the position to shower the enemy with arrows while their spear-armed comrades fought. If the heavy infantry advanced to storm a fortified position or breach, they would also be covered by archers whose job it was to pick off defenders attempting to venture close.

Chariots were usually deployed on the flanks or in front of the infantry positioned in the centre. Apart from screening the deployment of the infantry, chariots employed archery to disrupt the enemy formation or sought to destroy it by attacking head-on. Chariot attacks were mostly conducted in concert with the cavalry and were designed to break the enemy formation by sheer shock force. Such attacks were only carried out after the enemy had been pelted with missiles and seriously weakened, or on an already wavering line in order to achieve a breakthrough or rout. Depending on the situation at hand, the chariots and horsemen would then direct their focus towards the enemy flanks. Assyrian reliefs show chariots engaging enemy infantry, cavalry, and chariots. Arresting the momentum of a chariot attack, for example by densely packed infantry employing massed polearms (as the Macedonians would later do), does not yet seem to have formed part of the tactical repertoire.

Cavalry would also operate independently. If the enemy stood firm, cavalry would attempt to circumvent the flanks and employ missiles to weaken the enemy centre from behind. However, such a strategy was promising only if the enemy chariots and horsemen had been driven off. Infantry would attempt to keep up with the cavalry and exploit any weakening of the enemy line. Sargonid cavalry no longer regularly employed shields but wore improved body armour.

Sources confirm that enemy armies also resorted to refined tactics. Tiglath-Pileser III writes in his account of his campaign against Rassunu of Damascus in 733–732 BC: "…and their battle order I destroyed." In his commentary on the battle of Elteqeh (Altaqu) Sennacherib remarks that "..on the plain of Altaqu [the enemy] deployed in battle order." When Esarhaddon fought his brothers for the throne, the two armies met at Malatya in 681 BC: "They saw my mighty battle order attack (…) Their firm ranks were scattered [by the goddess Ishtar].."

Assyrian pictorial sources do not depict concrete battle orders, and so many assertions regarding tactics must remain conjectural. Since the Egyptians are the only other more or less contemporary culture whose depictions of military affairs have come down to us, we are mostly forced to go by written accounts.

Egyptian pictorial sources offer at least some clues. Most of these date from the 13th and 12th centuries BC, but since military affairs did not change over-much in the following five hundred years, rudimentary conclusions concerning the Assyrian army are possible. The Egyptian army of the Ramesside era was composed of infantry and chariots, cavalry playing a comparatively minor role. A deployed Egyptian force as depicted on contemporary Egyptian reliefs would have consisted of a core of infantry surrounded by swarms of chariots in the van and rear, and on the flanks. The chariot teams' primary weapon was the bow.

Assyrian deployment was probably similar, with alternat-

---

49   Maces were employed to dispatch wounded enemies or even prisoners. Canes and clubs may have been used to exercise physical authority over captives or to instil troop discipline, while axes and hatches were frequently employed by engineers.

ing ranks of archers and heavily-armed infantry forming the army's centre, and these being surrounded by units of cavalry and chariots. Variations in battle order, for example to allow a concerted flank attack by chariots and cavalry, would have occurred according to the tactical situation at hand. It appears plausible that units of archers were deployed in separate blocks in the centre or ahead of the main line. It was however left to the spearmen to charge and engage the enemy in close combat.

Battle commenced with the charioteers and both the mounted and foot archers showering the enemy with arrows. In this they were joined by the slingers, the handling of whose weapons probably forced them to advance ahead of the main line. Archers and slingers would open up at long range, if conditions permitted. To avoid losses by friendly fire, the chariots and cavalry were probably positioned on the flanks at this stage.

If the Assyrians were lucky, the enemy might already break under this hail of missiles. If the opposing lines stood firm, chariots and cavalry were launched against them in several successive waves. Horsemen and charioteers would engage any counterattacking cavalry and chariots with bows and javelins. If an enemy wing was routed, chariots and cavalry would attempt to take the enemy centre in the flank and rear, while the infantry pressed home their frontal attack. Sometimes chariots and cavalry would even take on the enemy infantry in a direct charge. Melées between the opposing chariot and cavalry forces seem to have been common. The Assyrians probably sought out weak spots in the enemy positions for attack, for instance allied troops which they suspected of being unreliable and therefore of low morale. In his account of the battle of Mount Uauš (Uaush) against the Urarteans and their allies under King Rusas I in 714 BC, Sargon reminisces: "With my own chariot alone, and with the horse guards, I shattered his centre like an arrow, causing his defeat and bringing his attack to a standstill. Like so many sheep I slaughtered at his feet his warriors, the mainstay of his troops, archers and spearmen, and cut off their heads". Sargon's victory was probably made possible by a concentrated attack by a few chariots and massed cavalry against the Urartean centre. The enemy broke either because of the surprise this caused, or because the Assyrian charge was directed at a weak point in the Urartean line, e. g. the junction between Urartean forces and allied contingents.

It is beyond doubt that Assyrian generals were perfectly capable of conducting simultaneous attacks directed both at the enemy's front and flanks. In 691 BC, Sennacherib campaigned against a coalition of Elamites, Chaldeans, Arameans and Babylonians. The two armies met at Halule: "I mounted my royal chariot...at my lord Ashur's command I charged the enemy's front and flank like a stormwind. With my lord Ashur's weapon [the bow] and the force of my attack I scattered them and put them to flight. I transfixed the enemy hosts with my own arrows." Above every stage of a battle rang shouted orders and the

sound of military instruments, either for deployment, exchange of missiles, cavalry and chariot attack, or infantry advance. Sargon II mentions orders for the advance, the retreat and the rallying of troops.

Cavalry and chariots returning from a missile attack on the enemy would regroup either on the infantry's flanks or in the rear [50]. While this was happening, the infantry archers would once again open fire on the enemy line. A chariot or cavalry charge could only be stopped by massed archery and missile fire, since these rapidly moving targets were extremely hard to engage. This succession of attacks would continue until the enemy broke. It is worth remembering that the effect a deploying Assyrian army with its large number of chariots had on enemy morale must already have been considerable.

While the cavalry and chariots were fighting, the infantry would move up in preparation for the final charge. Cavalry and chariots would pursue fleeing enemy troops and prevent them from rallying. Horsemen would employ archery and javelins during the pursuit, and use the lance at close quarters. The Taylor prism records Sennacherib's account of a concerted attack on the enemy's front and flanks during the battle of Halule in 691 BC. The king makes a point of stating that the Assyrians advanced shouting their feared war-cry: "Above the enemy ranks my war-cry resounded like a thunderstorm, and I bellowed like Adad the weather-god."

Was it the watchword shouted above the din of battle which kept friend and foe apart, or was it differing outward appearance? The sources neither show nor mention military uniforms, flags or standards to aid recognition. The Assyrians seem to have carried images of deities in the form of a Roman *vexillum* standard on some chariots, but the purpose of these was religious rather than tactical.

Although both acoustic and visual aspects seem to have played a role, it was probably mostly the common watchword that helped two forces distinguish between friend and foe in battle, the more so since it was common to have soldiers from one and the same nation fighting in two opposing armies. For example, in Assyria's wars against Elam, renegade Elamites could be found serving in the Assyrian ranks. Watchwords would have been the names of Assyrian gods, or the king's name.

When besieging a city or fortress, the Assyrians favoured not so much the strategy of starvation but normally chose to take the enemy walls by storm. Engineers would bring to bear Assyrian siege technology in the form of battering rams and siege towers. First however, the Assyrian general would attempt to capture the city by negotiation. If this proved impossible, the Assyrians would resort to psychological warfare: may reliefs show captives being impaled

---

50   This form of attack must have resembled the cavalry caracole of the Thirty Years War, in which cuirassiers and arquebusiers would attempt to disrupt the enemy line by a continuous discharge of pistols and carbines.

on stakes outside the city walls to induce terror and persuade the garrison or townspeople to surrender. Traitors or deserters were blinded or flayed alive. The aim of such appalling measures was to disrupt enemy alliances without too much loss of life on both sides, and to discourage emulation by any who happened to be considering joining in. Judging by the standards of the time the Assyrians were not even overly cruel; they were not interested in implementing a scorched-earth policy, since this would have prevented them from exploiting the defeated enemy's resources in the form of annual tributes, or from resettling the countryside with populations deported from other parts of the empire. If captured cities were destroyed, as was Babylon at the hands of Sennacherib, this was due to political strategy rather than to vengefulness. Nevertheless, strong fortifications such as those of Jerusalem were perfectly capable of withstanding even the most refined Assyrian siegecraft, and Sennacherib was finally forced to abandon his attempt to capture the city after a prolonged and costly siege.

In his report on his campaign against Jerusalem in 701 BC, Sennacherib does however mention the storming of numerous cities in the vicinity of the capital. These were less well fortified and quickly yielded to Assyrian attacks: "… and the small cities I besieged with wooden galleries and siege engines, through breaches, mines and engineers' tools, and by infantry attack".

The campaign against Urartu saw the Assyrians applying a scorched-earth policy after all. Large stretches of land were torched, cities and fortresses reduced to rubble, forests were cut down and channels filled in, fields and meadows were flattened, and everything even remotely useful was removed as plunder. Sargon II writes that the Urarteans had managed to warn the populations of the towns in the Assyrians' path of advance by a relay system of watch towers and fire signals, so that many settlements which would have been difficult to defend were evacuated on time without bloodshed.

If the Assyrians wished to surprise an enemy force, night marches were a common strategy. Any strategic information deemed necessary was gathered by a military intelligence service with the help of local governors, vassals, and a network of spies. At the time of Sargon II the military intelligence service was commanded by crown prince Sennacherib.

Command in battle

Even though Sargon II and Sennacherib relate personal feats of heroism on the battlefield, such boasts must be treated with caution. Assyrian generals including the king knew full well that a commander's place in battle was not necessarily in the front line but in a suitable place from where an army could be controlled effectively. In a letter to King Esarhaddon, an Assyrian court official writes: "The King, my Lord, ought not to hurl himself into the thick of the fighting, on the contrary. Stand on a hill like your ancestors and leave the conduct of the fighting to the generals".

If commanders chose to fight in person, it was to achieve surprise or to rally wavering troops by personal example. The death of Sargon II in battle against the nomads of the North proves that even high-ranking commanders were not above taking personal risks: a part of the royal army had been ambushed and the king hurried to the aid of his beleaguered troops, possibly without waiting for sufficient support from his household troops. Thus he became involved in the fighting and was eventually cut down.

Other, more subtle ruses were also popular. A long time before Sargonids, the Egyptian officer Amen-em-heb relates an episode from Thutmose III's (1479–1425 BC) campaign against the city of Kadesh: "The Prince of Kadesh sent a mare in heat amongst the Egyptian host. I followed her with my spear and sliced open her belly." Obviously the intention of the prince of Kadesh had been to inflict chaos among the Egyptian chariot teams. It is probably not wrong to assume the Assyrians capable of similar tricks.

Military terms, notes, and sources

Cuneiform inscriptions feature a number of military terms and phrases. Apart from weapons like spears, knives, swords, shields, slings, and maces, ranks and military functions are also named, e. g. shield-bearer, private soldier, cavalry troop leader, cavalryman etc. Vocabulary and phrases referring to weapons, fortress construction, an army on campaign and in camp are quite commonly found. In his commentary on the Assyrian campaign against Urartu and Muşaşir in 714 BC, Sargon II mentions pioneers wielding bronze and iron pickaxes, infantry, cavalry, chariots of the royal household, messengers, and the *hupsu* troops that followed in the wake of the afore-mentioned troops. Just what function these messengers and *hupsu* soldiers actually had, is slightly unclear. They might have been baggage attendants, or craftsmen such as blacksmiths, carpenters, and cooks. It is also possible that their ranks comprised military clerks, servants, camel and donkey drivers, and auxiliaries.

The Sargon Stele excavated at Kition in Cyprus records Sargon II's incorporation of 300 enemy chariots and 600 horse into his own army after his victory over king Yahu-bidi of Hamath. Sargon's own horse guard was probably about 1 000 strong[51] and consisted of mounted archers and horsemen armed with shields and spears. This also may be deduced from the stele's inscription[52].

Apart from bows and lances, spears and axes are also mentioned. Reliefs also depict slingers and stone throwers, and warriors armed with swords and daggers. Oddly enough, depictions of soldiers actually employing their swords in combat are comparatively rare. Many Assyrian soldiers are shown armed with spears or lances besides their bows. This double armament constituted a considerable tactical advantage as it provided the Assyrian soldier with increased flexibility. While the bow was employed as a long-distance weapon on the attack and in pursuit as well as during sieges, spear and lance were used in combat at close quarters. A soldier's expert use of several weapons required prolonged and thorough training.

Of course, the professional soldiers were better equipped than the levies. Pictorial sources clearly depict differences in equipment without providing specific information as to the troop type shown. Well-armed, well-dressed soldiers are shown alongside lightly-equipped warriors in simple garb. It is surely safe to assume that the royal household troops received the best equipment available. These are normally depicted surrounding the general or the king himself and are usually equipped with helmets and corselets. Lightly equipped troops may also be regulars, but it is also possible that they are vassal troops or levies. The latter could also be more heavily equipped of course, the equipment being the soldier's share of the spoils of war, or a reminder of his one-time professional army career. Equipment may therefore not be categorized as a distinguishing feature regarding the soldier's unit or social or ethnic origin. On the contrary, differences in armour and equipment seem to have gradually diminished over time. Soldiers from different nations differed mainly in their costume and the manner in which they wore their hair and beards. Assyrian guardsmen are frequently shown wearing corselets and conical helmets, and the characteristic military boots, but a simple diadem or headband could also be worn in place of a helmet. Some of these soldiers also differ in the size and form of their shields, which may indicate different household regiments.

A distinguishing piece of equipment for officers and guardsmen seems to have been the mace. This weapon often sported a spiked head in the mediaeval manner, and a leather band tied around the handle with which to secure it around the soldier's wrist. Some officers and household troops also carried canes. Officers were recognizable by the superior quality of their dress and equipment, and by the jewellery that was frequently worn. The armbands and bracelets shown on reliefs may have been decorations awarded for bravery.

---

51 In his account of his campaign against the small kingdom of Muşaşir, he claims only to have employed his personal chariot and 1 000 household cavalry.

52 In his campaign against the small princedom of Musasir, Sargon claims to have only taken one chariot and his horse guards. He mentions altogether 1 000 horsemen

sāb šarri	"The King's Men"	*rab šāqê*	chief cup bearer
kiṣir šarrūti	professional soldiers of the standing army	*rab ša rēšē*	(also *rab šaris*) chief eunuch
		rab bēti	steward
ša šēpē	household troops, guards	*šaknu*	prefect
ša qurbūte	personal bodyguards of the king and his family, also employed on special missions and as royal messengers	*chanu*	adjutant (?)
		rab mūgi	high-ranking commander of chariots, cavalry, or infantry
mutēr pūti	cf. *ša qurbūte.* This was probably merely a different name for the king's personal retainers; it only appears in Neo-Assyrian contexts.	*šalšu kiššati*	commander of three units
		rab kašzi	commander of archers
		amelša biṯḫallē	(also *rab pēṯḫal*) commander of horse
kiṣru	cohort	*mušarkisu*	recruiting officer
pēṯḫal	horseman (sg.), cavalry (pl.)	*rab ešerte*	NCO commanding a section of 10 soldiers
zukū	infantry		
turtānu	field marshal	*rab ḫanšī*	captain commanding 50 soldiers
sukkali	vizier	*rab kišir*	cohort commander
sartennu	chief justice, supreme judge	*rab urâte*	officer (function unspecified)
masennu	treasurer	*bēl pīḫati*	governor
nāgir ekalli	royal herald		

COMPOSITION, STRUCTURE, AND TECHNOLOGY OF THE ASSYRIAN ARMY

Chariot crews consisted of the driver, an archer, and a shield-bearer (at the time of Ashurbanipal there were two of the latter). The infantry consisted of archers, heavy infantry armed with spears and lances, and slingers[53]. Cavalry troopers were either armed with the bow or as medium cavalry with spear and lance. These troops were complemented by engineers and sappers with all the equipment of their trade. Since an army marches on its stomach, the military baggage attendants and transport troops responsible for the baggage animals such as oxen, camels, mules, dromedaries and donkeys also formed an essential part of the Assyrian army.

A significant role was played by the horses. The chariot teams were invariably stallions, mostly from the northern and north-eastern parts of the Assyrian empire, or acquired as part of annual tributes. The young, unbroken horses had to undergo a time-consuming period of training before they could begin to perform their role as chariot horses or cavalry mounts. Instructions for military horse care and training survive in form of clay tablets from the Middle Assyrian period, but unfortunately the surviving material is only fragmentary. Nevertheless we learn that the procedures involving the acclimatization, breaking in and training of military horses were strictly regularized. The earliest instructions regarding the breeding and training of military horses have come down to us from the Hittites, who normally envisaged a period of 185 days to fully train a military mount according to its future employment. The distances the horses were made to cover at different speeds under varying conditions were gradually extended. The considerable day's distance of 150 kilometres could normally only be achieved under training conditions. On campaign, a horse carrying a fully equipped cavalryman would have been able to cover between 60 and 80 kilometres under favourable conditions. It was common to expose the animals to heat and thirst by covering them with blankets and limiting the amount of drinking water. In spite of these hardships, the horses were excellently taken care of by their grooms, they were bathed, oiled and salved, and given the best fodder available.

Since the more cumbersome chariots were susceptible to the effects of coarseness of the terrain, they were not usually able to cover the same distances as the cavalry. Cavalry and chariots always operated together; thus it was the chariots which determined the daily distance covered, and the speed at which this happened. Normal marching speed would have amounted to between 8 and 12 km/h. If chariots and cavalry marched as part of the main army instead of scouting or raiding, the rate of march would have been determined by the infantry and the baggage train.

Judging from pictorial sources and bone finds, Assyrian horses resembled modern Arab horses, which are a sturdy and tough breed. Whether other breeds, for example from the vast steppes north of the Caucasus were used, is impossible to tell. The Assyrians acquired most of their horses from the Syrian-Hittite kingdoms, Urartu, the princedoms of Mannea and Tabal, Parsua, and from the Medes. The latter were also the main suppliers of camels. Large horses from Gilzanu were especially popular.

In his account of the campaign against Urartu, Sargon II describes the origins and training of horses from the northern lands. He remarks that these still had to be trained to attack at a gallop, to wheel, and to retire in order to regroup.

---

53 All of these warriors carried secondary armament, e. g. swords, daggers, maces, and hatchets. Many also wore helmets and body armour, and carried shields. The broad military belt was universally worn.

Guardsmen and chariot

Austen Henry Layard, *A Second Series of Monuments of Nineveh*, plate 24 (page 38).
Digital library, University of Heidelberg.

The relief forms part of the Lachish cycle. It depicts Sennacherib's chariot surrounded by guardsmen. A fortified camp can be seen at top right. Inside, Assyrian priests, recognizable by their mitre-like caps, perform a ritual in front of a chariot carrying sacred images. It was common to mount standards with images of deities on chariots. In this way, the gods would accompany the king and his army on campaign and provide both blessing and divine protection.

Siege tower

Austen Henry Layard, *The Monuments of Nineveh*, plate 17 (page 46).
Digital library, University of Heidelberg.

This relief from Nimrud shows King Ashurnasirpal II in royal regalia during a siege. The siege engine has an incorporated tower from which archers provide cover for the battering ram at work on the wall.

Assyrian troops crossing a river

Austen Henry Layard, *A Second Series of Monuments of Nineveh*, plate 41 (page 55).
Digital library, University of Heidelberg.

This relief is from Nineveh and dates from the reign of Ashurbanipal. Assyrian armies frequently had to cross rivers in full flood. Barges *(kelek)* were used to ferry heavy equipment, while the troops used inflated animal hides. The soldiers would carry their equipment on their backs.

King Ashurnasirpal II crosses a river

Austen Henry Layard, *The Monuments of Nineveh*, plate 15 (page 44).
Digital library, University of Heidelberg.

Relief from the palace of Ashurnasirpal II in Nimrud. The method of crossing rivers with keleks or boats and inflated animal skins had been in use at least since the reign of Ashurnasirpal II 200 years previously. Horses were made to swim, while baggage wagons, chariots and other important equipment were ferried across in boats.

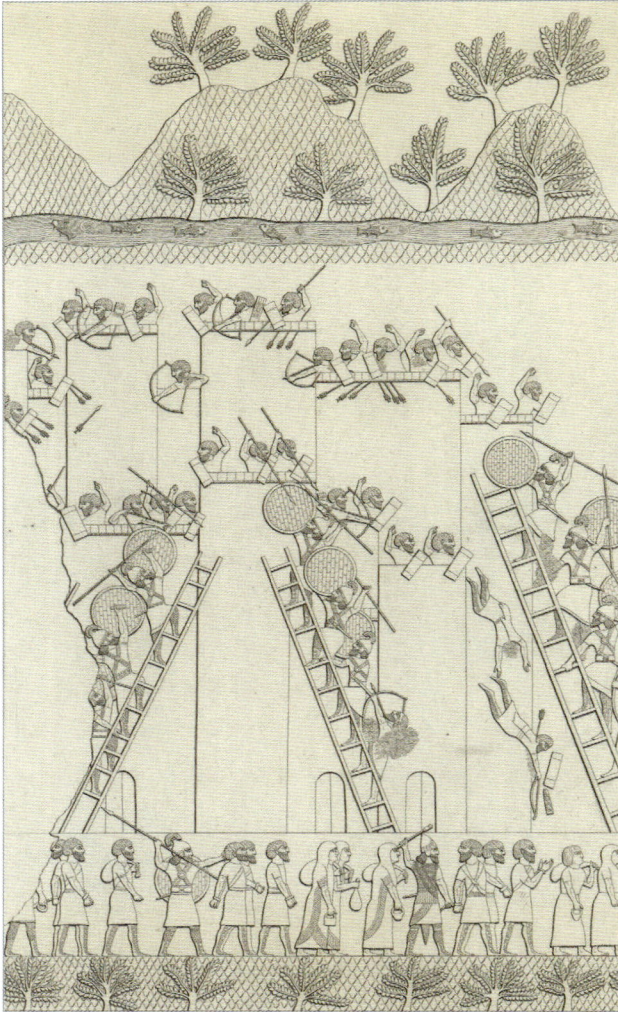

Assyrian troops storm a city

Austen Henry Layard, *The Monuments of Nineveh*, plate 68 (page 97).
Digital library, University of Heidelberg.

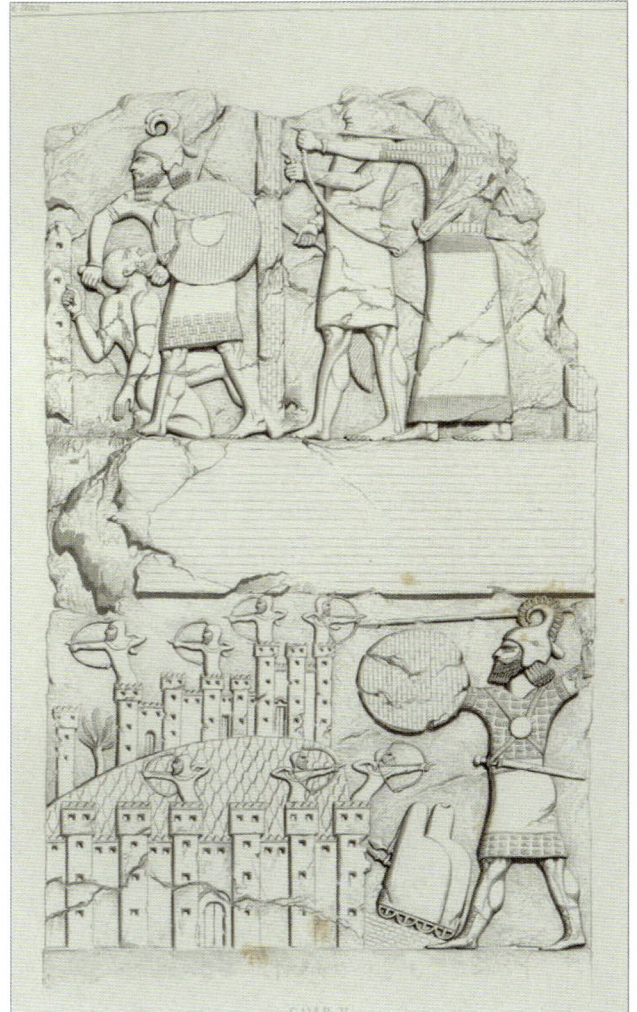

Besieging a walled city

Paul-Émile Botta, *Monument de Ninive*, vol. 2, plate 90 (page 10).
Digital library, University of Heidelberg.

The walls of a city situated to the north or north-east of Assyria are assaulted by Assyrian troops scaling the walls with the help of ladders. The Assyrian soldiers wear conical, crested or ridge helmets, bronze or leather belts, and lamellar cuirasses or round breastplates. They are further distinguished from the defenders by their round shields, those of the enemy being rectangular. The defenders are shown unarmoured, which is probably artistic convention since we can assume that the men manning the walls were likewise armoured. Their armament is similar to that of the Assyrians. The high boots and the hairstyle worn by the defenders permits geographical identification of the besieged city as being situated in the north, where there was an abundance of horses.

In order to breach enemy walls, which were mostly constructed of unkilned clay bricks, the Assyrians could choose from several methods. Walls were frequently only veneered up to a certain height, the upper sections and battlements often leaving the brickwork exposed. The warrior in the foreground wears a crested helmet and a tunic covered with small iron or bronze plates. To what extent these tunics possessed protective qualities, remains a matter of debate. Possibly the artist merely wished to show a particularly elaborate form of textile pattern. The crest material is difficult to identify – feathers, animal hair or bronze plumes appear possible. The warrior wears a round chest protector and covers himself with a wickerwork shield.

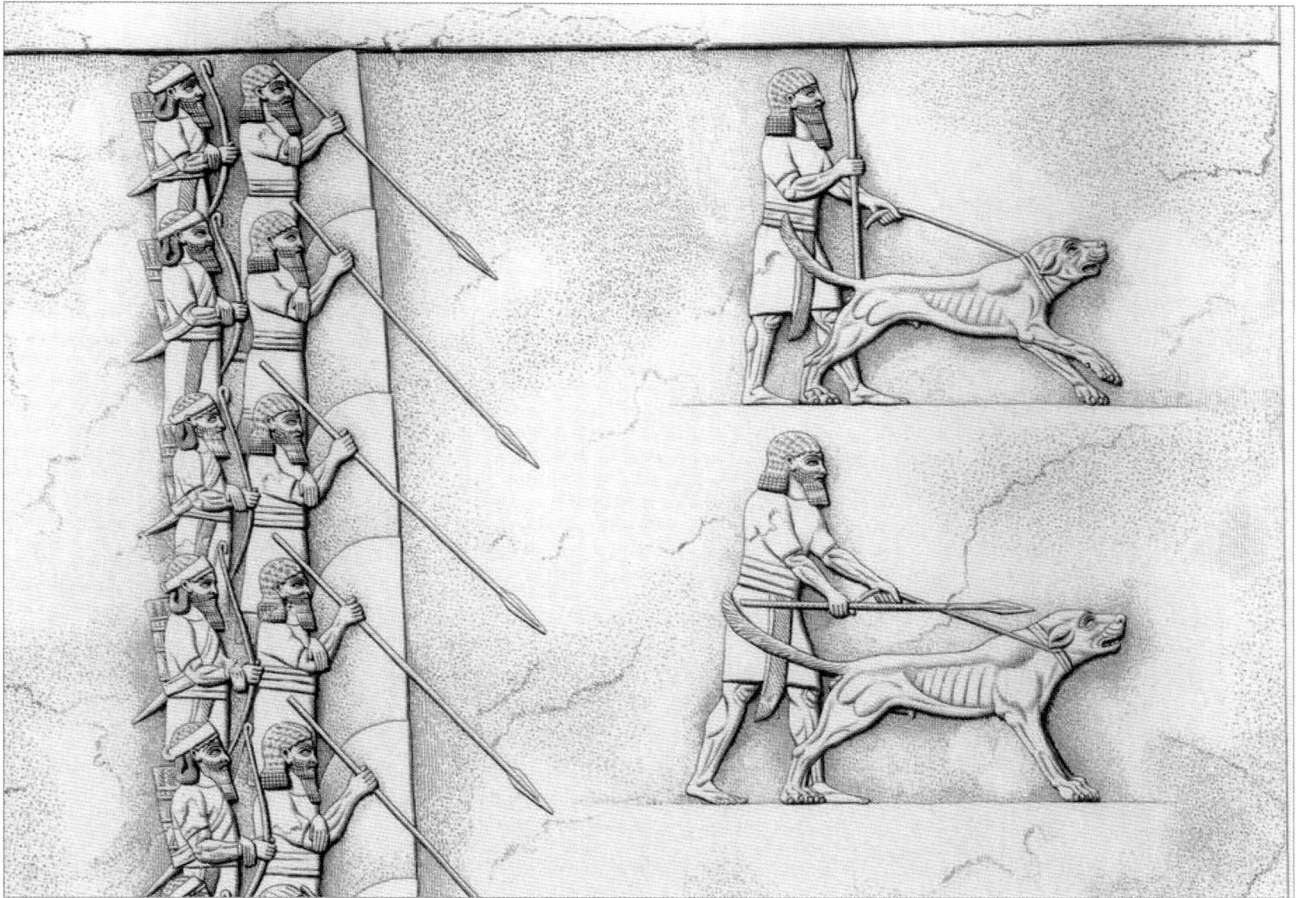

Dog handlers

Victor Place, *Ninive et l'Assyrie*, vol. 3, plate 51 (page 56).
Digital library, University of Heidelberg.

Although the relief depicts a hunting scene, a line of archers has taken up position behind the dog handlers together with their accompanying shield bearers. Dogs were used not just for hunting.

Assyrian horse guards

Paul-Émile Botta, *Monument de Ninive*, vol. 2, plate 143 (page 65).
Digital library, University of Heidelberg.

The relief was found in room VIII of Sargon II's palace in Khorsabad. Only a small number of reliefs were still in place in the room, among them a panel showing the sack of the temple at Mushashir. The other reliefs probably also depict scenes from the campaign of 714 BC. The panel at hand presumably depicts soldiers of Sargon II's horse guard. Reliefs from the Sargonid period frequently show horsemen clad in similar garb and with identical equipment forming part of the royal retinue.

Chariots

An Assyrian chariot was commanded by the first shield-bearer. A second shield-bearer, who was added at the time of Ashurbanipal, further helped to protect the crew from enemy missiles. All charioteers were trained in the use of the bow, thus enabling the crew to support the infantry archers with their fire at the beginning of a battle. Supplementary bows were stowed in cases attached to the chariot's sides.

The chariot was equipped with bows, javelins and spears for use at different ranges. In his *letter to Assur* from the year 614 BC Sargon II writes that at Mount Uauš the horses of King Rusas' chariot team were killed by arrows and spears.

Chariot crews could dismount and fight on foot, but this was usually only done if the chariot overturned or was otherwise damaged. Weapons for this eventuality were kept in cases attached to the chariot's cab (see below). It was probably the shield-bearers' job to prevent their fellow crewmen from being thrown off the chariot at high speed. To maintain a firm footing, the soldiers were also able to hold on to ropes attached to the inside of the cab.

The amount of armour worn by chariot crews varied. Early reliefs show chariot crews wearing coats of lamellar armour reaching down to their ankles. Helmets were equipped with scale aventails or coifs protecting the wearer's neck, throat, and shoulders. During the Sargonid period, only engineers retained this kind of heavy armour. Charioteers no longer seem to have worn it.

Most chariots at this time were drawn by teams of two or four horses[54]. Since Assyrian reliefs invariably show chariots in profile, it is often difficult to determine the exact number of horses in a team. Mesopotamian chariots underwent significant developments in the course of time: pictorial sources from the early Neo-Assyrian period up to the reign of Tiglath-Pileser III show vehicles running on wheels with fairly small diameters and only six spokes. The axle was situated in the middle of the chariot body. After Tiglath-Pileser III's reign, wheels became significantly larger, reaching almost the height of a man under Ashurbanipal. The wheels, which now had eight spokes, received metal tyres. The chariot's axle moved to the back of the vehicle to improve both manoeuvrability and the crew's balance. The wooden chariot pole was attached to the bottom of the cab with a metal sleeve and slanted upwards diagonally to end in a yoke for the horses (exact details as how the different chariot components were joined are lacking since in the reliefs the horses obscure the relevant areas). Yokes were padded and tied with leather. The horses were harnessed to the flexible yoke with leather thongs, providing the traction force by means of chest straps.

The position and run of the reins was also modified to improve control of the horses. This was deemed necessary, because the number of horses in a chariot team was increased. Harnessing techniques varied, yokes existing both for teams of two and four. Sometimes only two horses were harnessed to the chariot pole, the outer two being outriggers.

The weight of an Assyrian war-chariot can only be assessed in theory. A heavy war-chariot capable of carrying four men would have weighed about 200 kilogrammes without its crew. Manned by four fully equipped warriors, the chariot's weight would have amounted to between 450 and 500 kilogrammes.

Chariots were mostly constructed of wood. Metal was used to join parts of the chariot's cab, wheels, axle and pole. The cab itself consisted of a wooden frame covered with leather or wicker to reduce weight. The wickerwork was covered with hide, and occasionally bronze scales or studs were attached to protect the crew's legs and genitals. To facilitate transport, Assyrian chariots could be dismantled and reassembled in a fairly short amount of time. Just like cavalry horses, the teams wore protection in the form of peytrals and trappings, some horses were equipped with chamfroms. Bowcases and quivers storing arrows or javelins were attached to the sides of the cab, as were axes and spears for close combat. Some chariots are depicted carrying standards – of this more anon.

The chariot's combat value depended on the nature and composition of the terrain. War-chariots required space and hard, flat terrain to manoeuvre effectively. Maximum speed probably amounted to between 30 and 40 kilometres per hour, but could only be briefly sustained so as not to exhaust the horses.

The chariots' tactical value rested with the speed and manoeuvrability with which archers could be brought into favourable shooting positions, and the demoralizing effect a massed chariot attack could have on the enemy. Chariots advancing out of a huge cloud of dust accompanied by the thunder of hooves and the clash of weapons must have proved an unnerving experience even for the most experienced troops. Chariot attacks aimed at breaking enemy formations by sheer shock force after preceding missile attacks by archers and javelineers. If the attack succeeded, the centre of the enemy infantry would be attacked in the flanks and the rear. Cavalry and chariots also served to protect the Assyrian infantry from similar attacks by the enemy. Chariots were employed for reconnaissance missions and would pursue a fleeing enemy to prevent regrouping. Chariots could also be used to transport infantry during raids or surprise attacks. A little similar to modern dragoons, the foot soldiers would dismount to attack a settlement or engage an enemy formation. Modern scholars presume that a fully turned out Assyrian army could cover a maximum of 22 kilometres per day on the march. Some unconfirmed sources imply that chariots were organized into groups of ten. This sophisticated system would have necessitated a large amount of officers

---

54   For details see Wolfgang Nagel's work Der mesopotamische Streitwagen und seine Entwicklung im mediterranen Bereich (Berlin, 1966).

Assyrian chariot

Paul-Émile Botta, *Monument de Ninive*, vol. 1, plate 76 (page 85).
Digital library, University of Heidelberg.

The relief from Sargon II's palace at Khorsabad shows an Assyrian chariot in action. The exact number of horses is impossible to tell since Assyrian sculptors invariably show chariots in profile. The type of chariot depicted was probably drawn by a team of four, despite the fact that only three horse crests are visible. The crew consists of the chariot driver, an archer, and a shield bearer. The soldiers wear pointed helmets. This type of helmet is also visible on the wall paintings at Til Barsip.

Following double spread

Assyrian chariot

The chariot is drawn by a team of four. The horses are harnessed to the leather-bound yokes in horse-collar fashion. The wheels are bound with iron tyres. The chariot's construction represents the highpoint of Assyrian chariot development, which occurred during Ashurbanipal's reign. Although intended to accommodate a crew of four, it probably often only carried three soldiers for reasons of economy and speed. The barded horses wear leather trappings against enemy missiles and the crests frequently shown on Assyrian reliefs. The crest was presumably intended not just for display but together with a padded leather diadem also provided a certain amount of protection. The leather trappings were extremely hot and uncomfortable and were probably only worn for the shortest possible time to prevent the horses overheating. The chariot depicted is a commander's vehicle, recognizable by the standard emblazoned with the image of the weather god Adad. The standard normally remained in camp and was only mounted on the chariot by the priests when action was imminent.

The crew wear lamellar cuirasses and different helmet types. The archer wears a conical helmet while his comrades wear crested helmets. Corselets and helmets of iron were probably also worn. The chariot driver relies on his comrade's bronze circular shield for protection. During Ashurbanipal's reign, the chariot arm was already in a state of steady decline. This was chiefly due to economic aspects, but the unwieldy chariots were also proving increasingly unsuitable for the tactical requirements of the day. By this time, chariots only played a significant role in the flat terrains of Egypt and the Syrian and Mesopotamian plains.

and NCOs as well as standards and trumpet calls to maintain order and cohesion. As the Assyrian empire expanded and armies extended their reach, theatres of war shifted away from the deserts and plains to mountainous, boggy and wooded areas where the chariot was of little value. Enemies such as the Medes, Cimmerians and Scythians whose agile mounted archers were capable of running rings around the comaparatively cumbersome Assyrian war chariots became a serious problem. Chariot troops were therefore increasingly supplemented and eventually all but superseded by cavalry. Cavalry troops were also much cheaper to maintain and easier to train than charioteers and their teams. By the time the Assyrian Empire collapsed, the chariots had ceased to be a decisive factor on the battlefield. While reliefs from the time of Ashurnasirpal II and Sargon II still show chariots fairly often, sources from the reigns of Sennacherib and Ashurbanipal only show chariots as command vehicles (although this may be attributable to the specific situation depicted). The chariot as a weapon in the Middle East disappeared in the wake of the Greek and Persian and Macedonian Wars. Even when armed with the fearsome scythe blades rotating on their wheelhubs, Persian chariots stood no chance against the massed *sarissai* pikes of the Macedonian phalanx. They were last employed in the battle of Gaugamela in 331 BC. Henceforth, the use of chariots was limited to formal occasions.

Cavalry

The Assyrian cavalry had its heyday during the reigns of Sargon and Sennacherib, when their number was greatly increased. Up to this time, Assyrian cavalry had operated in pairs, a team consisting of a mounted archer and a spearman who held the reins while the archer operated his bow and provided the necessary cover with his shield. Reliefs at the royal palace at Khorsabad from the time of Ashurnasirpal II already show horsemen equipped with spears, shields and bows however. It appears plausible that inspired by Cimmerians, Scythians and Medes, the Assyrians had improved their horsemanship and were now able to do without the old division of combat roles. This would have meant that instead of one horseman out of every two being armed with a bow there were now two. This was an enormous increase in firepower since it doubled the amount of arrows the Assyrian cavalry was capable of firing at the enemy at any one time. Conversely, the archers were now also equipped and trained with the lance, many also adopting a shield. After firing his arrows, the cavalryman would now charge and engage the enemy at close quarters. Again this meant a doubling of Assyrian combat strength – after engaging the enemy at long range, the entire cavalry would close in and continue the fighting hand to hand. It can be assumed that at least for a certain amount of time enemy armies were incapable of dealing effectively with such tactical flexibility, and were not as well-armed.

A second cavalry branch were the medium cavalrymen equipped with helmets, corselets, spears and bows capable of mounting full-scale shock charges with the aim of breaking an enemy formation head-on. Assyrian cavalry would charge both infantry and cavalry, but could also act as skirmishers. It is quite surprising that Layard does not seem to have found a single relief at Nineveh showing Assyrian cavalry armed with shields. Obviously the cavalry abandoned the unwieldy shield and relied solely on their improved body armour for protection. Ashurbanirpal's cavalry decked their horses with bardings of leather or cloth joined and fastened by leather straps.

Regular Assyrian cavalry differed from levies, allies and mercenaries mainly in their equipment. Most were equipped with helmets and cuirasses. Since stirrups were as yet unknown[55], swords were not normally used for slashing, as this would have risked unbalancing the rider. Cavalry swords were also fairly short. Lances were not employed in the couched position so popular with mediaeval knights at tournament, but wielded overarm.

In order to secure the supply of suitable cavalry mounts, campaigns and raids were carried out by Assyrian troops into Urartean and Mannean territory, and into the steppes of north-western Iran, one of the centres of Median horse breeding. Especially Sargon II was fond of this manner of horse acquisition. Horses from the above-mentioned ar-

---

55   The first stirrups appeared in India around the year 50 BC.

Previous page:

Assyrian mounted archer and foot soldier

The mounted archer is from a medium cavalry unit and equipped with conical helmet and iron lamellar cuirass. The horse wears a cloth or leather barding. The padded headband is both ornament and protection. The rider's helmet is frequently shown on Sargonid bas-reliefs. But since iron finds from this period are extremely rare, this reconstruction is based on bronze examples. Many sources, especially from the time of Ashurbanipal's reign, show horsemen armed both with bow and lance.

The light infantryman only wears a headband, a bronze breastplate and a broad leather belt for protection. He is using a short curved sword to dispatch a fallen enemy. Heads were cut off and collected in order to assess the number of fallen enemies. Scribes recorded the number of trophies, which were then piled up to form a gruesome victory sign, serving both as a deterrent and proof of the Assyrian commander's military prowess. The number of heads taken may also have played a role in the distribution of booty among the soldiers.

Opposite page:

Assyrian cavalryman equipped with bow and lance

There was probably no clear distinction between light and medium (or heavy) cavalry. Troops were deployed according to strategic requirements and availability. Mercenaries and guardsmen were probably more lavishly equipped than simple levies. The cavalryman in the background is equipped in a manner depicted on numerous reliefs, many of them from the reign of Ashurbanipal. He wears a helmet and lamellar corselet and is armed with bow and lance. His horse is protected by a cloth or leather barding.

The cavalryman tending to his dying horse has removed his bronze helmet, which is based on a mural at the royal palace of Tel Ahmar (Til Barsip). Its blue colour actually indicates iron. The helmet itself differs in shape from standard Assyrian helmets of the Sargonid era. Its lower edge flares out into a neckguard. The crest knob was riveted to the top of the helmet. The cloth or leather lining was either sewn or glued to the inside of the helmet bowl.

Following double spread:

Armoured Assyrian cavalry

The plate shows various forms of body armour worn by the cavalry. The horsemen wear lamellar and scale corselets. The latter had been in use in Egypt and the Middle East for centuries. The lamellar corselets differ in the form of the plates used in their manufacture, one consisting of small rectangular plates instead of the small scales more commonly employed. The rows of lamellae, which could be bronze or iron, are interspersed with panels of the corselet's basic material, which was either leather or occasionally fabric. Reliefs from the time of Ashurbanipal show cavalrymen armed with bows and lances. Mounted archers and spearmen also seem to have existed. Horses wore bronze peytrals or strips of lamellar armour for protection, chest protectors made of leather studded with metal or padded fabric also existed. This can be deduced from the pictorial sources. Whether the ornamental trappings depicted on numerous reliefs such as animal pelts and decorative cords and tassels were also worn on campaign remains impossible to tell.

Horse peytrals
Austen Henry Layard, *The Monuments of Nineveh*, plate 32 (page 61).
Digital library, University of Heidelberg.

Peytrals served decorative and protective purposes. Decorations employing religious motives invoked divine support. Some peytrals consisted of several parts and existed in a variety of forms. Similar to a lamellar corselet, connected rows of armour provided increased protection. The relief at hand was found at Nimrud and was created long before the Sargonid period.

Bronze horse peytral

Badisches Landesmuseum Karlsruhe,
photograph by Peter Graul

Breadth: 35, 2 cm, height 34, 4 cm.

Since no Assyrian horse peytrals have been found, we choose to depict a Urartean example. It is of bronze manufacture with wrought and chased decorations. Peytrals like this one were sewn onto leather mountings, as can be seen by the holes to accommodate the stitching. The peytral is decorated with religious motives and depicts a Urartean deity receiving sacrificial gifts from a winged genius and a priest, or possibly the king himself. Excavated Urartean peytrals have been dated by scholars to around 800 BC.

eas habitually formed part of the annual tributes due to the Assyrian court. Every year, military officials took stock of the number of horses available to the Assyrian military. Reports also commented on the serviceability of the horses. Clay tablets from the years 710 to 708 BC listing the number of military mounts available have been found at Kalḫu (Nimrud). The battles of Halule (690 BC), Til Tuba (653 BC) and Ulai (652 BC) were all won by the Assyrian cavalry.

Infantry

The Assyrian infantry was made up of archers, slingers, and soldiers armed with spears and shields. Hatchets, maces, swords and daggers were used for close-quarter fighting. Individual soldiers differed mainly in the form and amount of equipment, e. g. helmets and body armour. Heads were also protected by headbands, diadems and caps made of leather or fabric. Shields differed in form, size and manufacture. All of this resulted in many different combinations of equipment, giving Assyrian soldiers a fairly motley appearance (with the possible exception of the household troops). Unfortunately, the amount of variations depicted by Assyrian sculptors is quite limited. This was presumably mostly due to the contemporary technical limitations to their craft, nevertheless auxiliaries, allies and enemies of the Assyrian army are clearly recognizable by their clothing, hairstyles, and beards.

Assyrian infantry sought to weaken the enemy by long-range missile fire before mounting a frontal attack. The primary weapon in close-range combat was the spear. Modern experiments have shown that Assyrian archers were capable of loosing between six and ten arrows per minute. Quivers held up to 30 arrows, implying that the first phase of an engagement, exposing the enemy to hail of arrows, only lasted about five minutes. There is no evidence for Assyrian archers being resupplied with arrows during a battle. If we assume that an Assyrian army had a contingent of about 10 000 archers (which is quite realistic), then the number of arrows fired at the enemy at the beginning of a battle would amount to no less than 300,000. The traction force when operating an Assyrian bow varied between 45 and 80 N depending on construction and condition of the weapon. Archers wore bracers of bronze, fabric or leather to protect their forearms from the rebounding bowstring. A skilled slinger could hit a target at a distance of 300 metres.

Engineers, craftsmen and siege technology

Due to the sieges which formed part of many a campaign, the Assyrian army contained a large proportion of pioneers, sappers, engineers and craftsmen who specialized in siege technology and the construction of the siege engines which form a prominent part of so many Assyrian reliefs. Siege engines were constructed locally since their sheer size would have rendered the army virtually immobile if they had been carried along in the baggage train. The main construction material was wood. Siege towers were covered with dampened animal hides to protect them from enemy missiles and firebrands. Essential siege technology comprised battering rams on wheels, and siege towers. A weapon frequently depicted was a battering ram swinging from a crossbar and equipped with a large spear-shaped head. This was especially suitable for breaching city walls typically constructed of unkilned clay bricks, and the layer of kilned bricks commonly used to veneer them. Rams with blunt heads were also employed. Some siege towers actually comprised two rams at different levels and other machinery to damage the walls and keep the defenders' heads down. Combined battering rams and siege towers frequently sported platforms from which archers maintained a sustained fire to clear the enemy walls of defenders and protect the crews manning the rams. Fire crews were kept ready in case a machine caught fire. The Lachish reliefs clearly show Assyrian engineers ladling water from the top of a siege tower to keep its outer surface damp and maintain it fireproof. In order to move siege towers into position, it was often necessary to construct siege ramps. This involved moving enormous amounts of earth and rubble. Often Assyrian siege troops would rely on simpler means to capture a city, e. g. they would attempt to scale the walls with the help of ladders, or fire gates made of wood. Bitumen was a widely-known and popular incendiary. Reliefs frequently show Assyrian engineers preparing to set fire to enemy defences. The engineers and sappers were equipped with the tools of their trade. Reliefs show them wielding spades, hoes and axes, presumably of bronze or iron. These tools were used to undermine the walls of a city with the aim of collapsing them. Sometimes mines were dug and then fired in order to collapse a stretch of wall or a tower. In his account of his campaign against King Hezekia of Judah in 701 BC, Sennacherib writes: "Forty-six of his walled cities and countless small towns surrounding them I besieged with wooden galleries and siege engines, through breaches, mines and engineers' tools, and by infantry attack".

A peculiar piece of armour worn by Assyrian soldiers even before the Sargonids was a long, gown-like scale corselet reaching to the ankles. These were issued to charioteers, and to engineers operating immediately below the walls of a besieged city in full view of the defenders, and within the range of enemy weapons. It was probably very difficult to protect these soldiers and their work with shields. Some reliefs do however show engineers equipped with

Previous page:

Assyrian infantry spearman

This Assyrian warrior with the typical hairstyle and beard wears a broad leather or textile headband studded with small bronze plates. Reliefs found at Dur Šarrukin, Nimrud and Nineveh show soldiers from different ethnic backgrounds wearing headbands or diadems of various shapes and sizes. These were not worn for protection but would instead have served as status symbols or unit identifiers. A relief from Nineveh dated to the reign of Ashurbanipal shows Assyrian warriors wearing the type of headdress depicted.

The warrior wears a fringed tunic in indigo blue with a richly decorated belt consisting of a broad belt of stout leather covered by a bronze belt on a leather or fabric backing. This type of belt can be found in numerous pictorial sources and is virtually identical with Urartean belts, of which several examples have been found. His other clothing consists of close fitting dyed hose made of wool, cotton, or linen. Wall paintings at the palace of Tel Ahmar (Til Barsip) show figures wearing hose only reaching to the upper thighs. When exactly the Assyrians adopted the more practical breeches worn by the Scythian, Median and Cimmerian nomad horsemen, remains unclear. The warrior's footwear consists of the typical Assyrian miitary boot, which was laced up at the back of the knee. Boots were laced up according to various fashions, as attested by different reliefs. The warrior is armed with a spear with an iron head and relies on a large oval wicker shield as his only protection. The shield is covered with leather and bound with bronze, and has a central boss. All bronze parts are embossed with rosette-shaped decorations as shown by several sources.

Opposite page:

Assyrian armoured spearman

This battle-scarred veteran belongs to a unit of heavy infantry. His rich equipment defines him as either a mercenary or a guardsman. He wears a bronze Assyrian conical helmet lined with leather. The helmet bowl with integrated cheekplates consists of two halves riveted together. It is based on an original find presented at an auction of Auktionshaus Hermann Historica, Munich, in 2019. A virtually similar example formed part of the exhibition at the Christoph Bacher Archäologie Ancient Art Galerie in Vienna. His lamellar corselet is made according to the latest military fashion and consists of iron scales mounted on a leather backing. Since only the scales have survived, the material of the backing is a matter of conjecture. The overlapping scales were probably sewn onto strips of leather. These strips were again sewn together so that they overlapped each other to form a complete corselet. An Assyrian relief of unusually good quality seems to imply this manufacturing method. The overlapping strips of leather between the rows of scales improved the corselet's protective quality considerably, since a double layer of leather together with the stitching was more difficult to penetrate than a single one. This type of corselet offered better mobility than more heavy types of scale body armour. The size of the scales varied according to manufacturer and their position on the armour. Smaller scales or lamellae were used to cover the area around neck and shoulders so as not to impede movement, and to accommodate the wearer's individual bodily features. Since however only very few examples of scales and lamellae from the Sargonid period have come down to us, a great deal of this reconstruction must needs be guesswork. Cuirasses were worn over the soldiers' tunics. Many had strips of leather attached around the waist to protect the genitals and the thighs, though some corselets only seem to have had these at the back.

As an alternative to the wickerwork shield, the soldier might also be carrying a wooden shield of plywood construction. The shield is covered with hide and edged with decorated bronze binding. This type of shield is the so-called "Egyptian" variant, also referred to as a tower shield. The warrior wears breeches or leggings, and the typical military boots. His sidearm is an iron sword with a bronze hilt in the form of a lion as depicted on numerous reliefs. His bracelets are probably booty from past campaigns. Like the sword, bracelets feature on several Assyrian reliefs and seem to have been popular among soldiers. To ward off the cold in the northern provinces (temperatures could drop to -5° C), he has donned a cloak of sheep's or goat's wool. The army of the Sargonids frequently campaigned in the north and in the mountains. The soldier's spear has a rounded iron spearhead. Finds confirm that a variety of shapes were common.

Assyrian foot archer

This archer wears a crested helmet. Several fragments of such helmets have survived, and they can frequently be seen on Assyrian triumphal reliefs. He wears a bracer on his left forearm, consisting of a decorated bronze plate attached to a leather armband. Such bronze plates have been found, and bracers like this can also be seen in Assyrian sculpture. The specimen illustrated belonged to a Urartean archer and formed part of the former Axel Guttmann collection, Berlin. The collection was dissolved after Guttmann's death in 2001, and items have since been integrated into various other collections worldwide. Other bracers merely consisted of leather wound or strapped around the archer's wrist.

The dagger is based on an iron example now at the British Museum. The lamellar corselet consists of bronze scales sewn onto a leather backing. Numerous iron and bronze scales have been found in various shapes and sizes. The leggings worn under the tunic are striped red and blue as worn by several soldiers on the murals found at the palace of Tel Ahmar (Til Barsip). The short tunics worn by several soldiers on the mural reveal that this form of legwear only extended up to mid-thigh. Since the archer is a member of an élite corps, he can afford a tunic of fairly expensive yellow dye.

Following double spread:

Assyrian slinger and infantry

Slinger

A slinger holds his ground under enemy fire during a siege. He wears an odd form of headdress based on an Assyrian relief. It has been reconstructed in the form of a round iron or bronze disc attached to a leather headband. Such disks were more commonly worn as chest protectors by horses and men. The slinger wears a lamellar corselet, tunic and leggings dyed in natural colours, and military boots. In this we follow Assyrian reliefs. His sidearm is a sword with a richly decorated lion-shaped hilt, though such an expensive weapon would normally have been beyond a simple warrior's means.

Shield-bearer

An Assyrian infantryman attempts to shield his comrade from the arrows loosed by the city's defenders. He wears a conical helmet with attached cheekpieces. The helmet has several embossed bands running around the base of the bowl for increased stability. His round shield is based on original finds from Luristan, and depictions in Assyrian sculptural art. Like the slinger, he too wears a lamellar cuirass. He is armed with a spear and a sword and wears striped leggings. The colours are conjectural. All colours and patterns in the illustrations follow the scant evidence, namely a few preserved coloured Assyrian reliefs, and take into account the production methods available at the time. Some aspects must remain guesswork however.

Assyrian foot soldier

Like his comrade he wears a conical helmet with embossed bands around the lower rim of the helmet bowl. Like bronze helmets, it was probably made of thin sheet metal. Unfortunately, finds of Assyrian iron helmets are extremely rare. The soldier wears a lamellar corselet with short sleeves. If one follows depictions of such armour on Assyrian reliefs, the sleeves were sometimes only covered with scales at the front. Possibly some corselets were only covered with scales at the front altogether, but there is no concrete evidence for this.

such heavy armour protected by a second man armoured likewise, and carrying a shield. Archers attempted to cover the work of the engineers and sappers with their fire, keeping the defenders' heads down.

The Assyrian army crossed rivers using barges (*kelek*) and rafts. Most soldiers simply swam using inflated animal hides (e. g. goat skins) to stay afloat. This is attested by numerous reliefs. King Shalmaneser II wrote in his account of the march to Damascus in 853 BC: "On ships of mutton-hide I crossed the Euphrates a second time."

It is striking that on most Assyrian reliefs there are significant differences between Assyrian and enemy troops regarding amount and standard of equipment. Most enemies appear poorly equipped despite the fact that archaeological finds show that this was by no means the case. Museums and private collections contain a large number of helmets and shields, many of them Urartean. Although finds are comparatively scarce, we may assume that Egyptian, Elamite, Babylonian, Chaldean, Aramean and Median armies were similarly well armed and equipped. All of these people were almost continuously at war with Assyria, which would have been impossible to sustain if they had not been sufficiently equipped and organized. Either the inaccurate depiction of enemy forces in Assyrian sculpture was done for propagandistic reasons, or the sculptors were simply ignorant of their actual appearance.

The baggage train

Assyrian reliefs and written sources feature horses, mules, donkeys and camels or dromedaries in the role of pack and draft animals. Since sufficient supplies could not be reliably obtained by foraging or plunder, it was important to provide for a large baggage train with supplies to keep the troops fed before setting out on campaign. Living off the surrounding country like a French Revolutionary army was not an option for Assyrian commanders. The amount of baggage animals must have been enormous even if one takes into account the weights which these animals were capable of carrying. A mule, for example, can carry ca. 140 kilogrammes over a reasonable marching distance, a donkey slightly less. If we calculate just one kilogramme's worth of rations per day for every soldier, an army numbering 60,000 men would have required 60 tons of supplies per day for the soldiers alone. Transporting three days' complete rations would have required 1,300 mules plus their drivers, not counting the livestock which provided the troops' meat rations. A cavalry or chariot horse required ca. 9 kilogrammes of fodder per day. If 10,000 horses had to be fed, this would have meant an extra 2,000 mules to transport the necessary supplies. The amount of other military equipment which had to be brought on campaign can only be guessed at, but it is safe to say that the baggage train of an Assyrian army in the field would have comprised a minimum of 6,000 baggage animals, not counting horses, camels, and the oxen who served as draft animals.

Since the functioning of logistics is a vital part of military administration regardless of circumstances, the Assyrian army must have had at its disposal a corps of officials and officers responsible for supplies, transport, and the necessary personnel. According to the sources, Sargon II was accompanied by large donkey and dromedary caravans on his campaign against Urartu in 714 BC. Carpenters and blacksmiths also accompanied the army on campaign. At night, fortified camps were constructed by the soldiers, whose work was supervised and supported by craftsmen and engineers.

Previous double spread:

Assyrian troops crossing a river

The geography of the Middle East, especially Mesopotamia itself, made it imperative for the Assyrian army to negotiate rivers. If we are to believe Assyrian royal accounts, armies were even capable of crossing rivers in full flood, a dangerous enterprise for man and beast with large rivers such as the Euphrates and the Tigris. Since river crossings were glorious and therefore memorable feats, they were commemorated in Assyrian triumphal art. Keleks were used to ferry across wagons, troops and animals (excluding horses); these boats have remained in use on the Tigris to this day. Horses were made to swim, and even some warriors chose or were ordered to swim across. Inflated animal hides were used to provide buoyancy, which was important in view of the fact that the soldiers were expected to carry their equipment on their backs. We cannot be sure if Assyrian soldiers were able to swim as a rule, and crossing a river in this manner was hazardous at the best of times. The plate shows a high-ranking Assyrian officer and his command chariot being ferried across a river. His magnificent iron helmet is covered with embossed, engraved and chased patterns and decorations. A similar bronze helmet is in the collection of the Museum zu Allerheiligen at Schaffhausen, Switzerland. The warrior standing behind the officer is equipped with a wicker shield covered with leather. The binding and boss are of metal. A standard decorated with the image of a deity has been mounted on the yoke.

DRESS, DYES, AND FABRICS

Assyrian textiles mainly consisted of linen, cotton, or wool[56]. Wool was mostly spun from goat, sheep or camel hair. Nobles wore silken garments, which were imported via India.[57] While cotton, wool, and silk can be dyed fairly easily, linen is difficult to dye, so that linen textiles were decorated by woven, stitched or even painted patterns. Byssus garments, which were made of finely woven linen, were highly prized possessions and given to high-ranking officials or generals as rewards. Cotton only became prominent during Sennacherib's reign. In his annals he boasts of having introduced to Assyria "the tree that bears wool". In spite of this, cotton had already been imported and received as tribute for a long time. Purple was used as a dye in the Neo-Assyrian period. It was gained from the Mediterranean purple dye murex and was capable of producing dark to light red, violet and purple dyes. It was however extremely expensive and therefore only affordable for a few privileged individuals. Purple fabrics were either imported or seized as spoils, or delivered as tribute to the Assyrian court. An apple-green intermediate dye was also used for garments, but this was not much more than a convenient by-product.

Washing and bleaching from the sun eventually changed a garment's original colour. This was of course also true for indigo, which was a popular dye in Mesopotamia.[58] Like modern denims, Assyrian clothing dyed with indigo would have appeared in all kinds of shades. Other dyes included saffron yellow[59], an expensive dye gained from crocuses, and madder red, a fairly affordable dark red dye gained from the plant of the same name (*rubia tinctorum*).[60] Depending on the quality of the plant material used and the temperature of the dye bath, madder produced dyes that could vary between dark red and orange, or brick red. Simple Assyrian warriors and civilians probably wore clothes in natural woollen or linen colours. Sheep wool would produce colours from white to various ochres, and brown or black. Linen would have come in ochres and light browns.

Some garments were decorated with applications that were applied to the fabric. Stitched-on borders and fringes added colour and variety to everyday clothing which might have appeared a little drab otherwise. Some soldiers will have possessed elabotate clothing which had been their share of a campaign's booty. Household troops would have been clothed more elaborately, if only for display. It is unfortunate that the few coloured murals depicting Assyrian clothing that have come down to us must be treated with caution. They were painted for effect rather than authenticity, and the artists had more natural colours and pigments at their disposal than there were dyes (e. g. coloured clays, metallic oxides, or rock flours). This, incidentally, also holds true for Egyptian mural and relief colours. Most coloured depictions have been found at the palace at Til Barsip (Tel Aḥmar, which means "red mound"), former capital of the Aramean princedom of Bit Adini. The murals were painted during the reigns of Tiglath-Pileser III and Shalmaneser V, both predecessors of Sargon II. The colours employed by the artists do not necessarily permit conclusions regarding the actual colour of Assyrian garments, since the paints were manufactured differently from contemporary dyes. For instance, some horses depicted on the Tel Aḥmar murals are painted in blue! It is not entirely clear whether this was done deliberately or constitutes the result of chemical processes which changed the colours to their present appearance. Be that as it may, it is obvious that coloured garments were a luxury in ancient Mesopotamia, a fact which becomes all the more clear if one considers that they are explicitly mentioned in sources recording tributes and booty.

In his accoint of his campaign in Palestine, Ashurnasirpal II (r. 883–859) lists the tributes delivered by the Phoenician cities who besides supplying him with numerous metals also provided the Assyrians with "garments and linen woven in bright colours". Assyrian sources referring to Ashurbanipal's Egyptian campaign make note of "brightly coloured [cotton?] and linen clothing". Sargon II's *Letter to Assur* mentions various textiles and dyes. At the sack of Muṣaṣir in 714 BC, the Assyrians seized garments with linen borders which were dyed in blue and and red [purple], and which were covered with small golden plates and embroidered with golden threads. These were the sacred vestments of the Urartean god Haldi, which the Assyrians robbed from the god's temple. It is clear that such priceless clothing was only worn by kings, princes and a few persons that ranked very high on the social ladder. Ashurbanipal observes in his account of the fighting against the Elamites that such was the slaughter that the waters of the river Eulaeus flowed "as red as wool".

---

56   Cotton was introduced to the Near and Middle East via India. Cotton finds in New Kingdom Egyptian tombs imply that the Assyrians also were familiar with cotton garments,al though they were probably rare. Assyrian sources make no reference to cotton, though wool is occasionally mentioned.

57   Silk was manufactured in China and India from the 3rd millennium BC.

58   The indigo plant (*genus indigofera*) originated from India. Its dye was already used in Egyptian mummy bandages from the time of the 5th dynasty (ca. 2500–2300 BC).

59   Saffron features in Akkadian cuneiform sources from the 2nd millennium BC. It too was used for dying Egyptian mummy bandages.

60   Madder was already being used as a dye during the 18th Egyptian dynasty (1552–1306 BC).

Mural from the palace at Til Barsip (Tel Aḥmar)

bpk images

The murals at Til Barsip were mostly painted during the reign of Tiglath-Pileser III (r. 745-726 BC), one of Sargon II's predecessors. We may assume that soldiers of the latter's army would have looked very much like the warriors depicted on the murals. The warrior leading the horses wears a pointed helmet, breeches or leggings, and high laced boots. He carries a whip in his left hand. The difference in the two warrior's height is remarkable; it appears that the artist wished to render a realistic idea of what the different soldiers actually looked like on campaign. One of the horses has a leopard skin for a saddle.

Mural from the palace at Til Barsip (Tel Aḥmar)

bpk images

The second mural shows an Assyrian warrior wearing a short tunic. He does not wear breeches but leggings which reach to mid-thigh reminiscent of modern hold-up stockings. This raises the question whether Assyrians actually wore stockings or breeches, and whether this depiction is an exception to the rule. Legwear is striped in red and blue, but this might merely be due to the colour of the paint availabe, and therefore not actually an authentic depiction.

Other legwear was probably single-coloured, or may have had different patterns and colour combinations. Other coloured depictions of Assyrian clothing are lacking as yet.

One of the warriors wields a curved sabre and wears conspicuously patterned clothing. Again individuals' heights vary. Note the elaborate pointed helmets.

94

Ceramic finds from Nimrud

Austen Henry Layard, *A Second Series of The Monuments of Nineveh*, plate 55 (page 69).
Digital library, University of Heidelberg.

The tile depicts the brilliantly coloured clothing worn by Assyrian nobles.

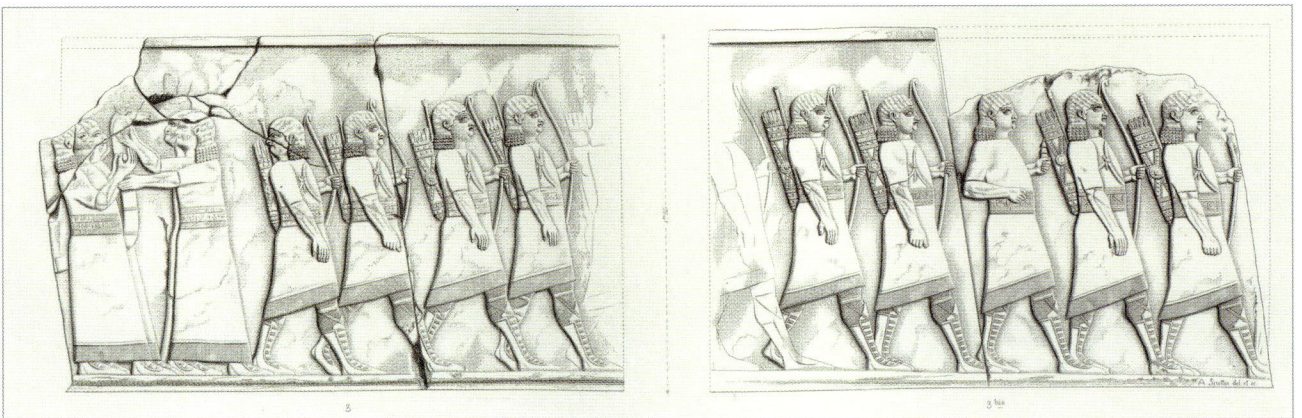

Assyrian Guardsmen

Victor Place, *Ninive et L'Assyrie*, vol. 3 (plates), plate 62 (page 78, bottom).
Digital library, University of Heidelberg.

The relief shows infantry archers on parade. They are clean-shaven (or beardless) and carry bows. They wear broad belts and circular breastplates. It is difficult to determine if these soldiers are eunuchs, or merely very young. In contrast to other reliefs, the chest-protectors are unusually large and cover the entire chest. The elaborately decorated clothing and equipment as well as the breeches and boots may point to a guard unit.

Assyrians besiege a city

Austen Henry Layard, *The Monuments of Nineveh*, plate 19 (page 48).
Digital library, University of Heidelberg.

The relief was found in the palace of Ashurbanipal II at Nimrud and depicts a siege involving Assyrian engineers or sappers clad in early gear.

The long armoured coats of the sappers at work on the walls and the warriors manning the siege tower no longer appear in triumphal art after the reign of Sargon II. The same is true of the coifs worn under the helmets. The defenders attempt to pull up the battering ram with the aid of a chain, a ruse which is being counteracted by two Assyrian soldiers equipped with long hooks. Fire crews sought to prevent the enemy setting fire to the siege engines, which were mostly constructed of wood.

Festive Assyrian clothing

Austen Henry Layard,
The Monuments of Nineveh, plate 9 (page 38).
Digital library, University of Heidelberg.

This picture is an artist's rendering of an Assyrian festive garment as depicted on a relief. Ornaments could be stitched, but metal applications sewn onto the fabric also seem to have been common.

Top:

Assyrian chariot

Alabaster relief, Vorderasiatisches Museum,
Staatliche Museen Berlin.
Photograph by Olaf M. Teßmer

This relief from the time of Ashurbanipal is from the South-Western Palace at Nineveh. The chariot carries a crew of four and was probably drawn by four horses.

Right:

Assyrian warriors with crested helmets and round shields

Alabaster relief, Vorderasiatisches Museum,
Staatliche Museen Berlin.
Photograph by Olaf M. Teßmer.
On display at the Pergamonmuseum, Berlin

This relief, which was also found at the South-Eastern Palace at Nineveh, is from the time of Sennacherib.

The Sargon Stele at Kition lists the king's spoils taken in the land of Hamath, among them garments dyed in red and blue purple. Not only cotton or linen were dyed, but also wool and the coats of domestic and wild animals. After his Syrian campaign in 738 BC, Tiglath-Pileser III was offered tributes of "sheep whose wool had been dyed with red purple", and "birds of the air whose feathers were the colour of violet purple".[61]

Especially in the colder regions of the Assyrian Empire, animal pelts and furs were in common use. Hides furthermore provided the leather for shoes, belts, straps and boots, but also for weapons, shields, sword and dagger sheaths, arrow quivers, corselets, and helmet linings. The main garment was the tunic, which could vary in length and cut, and which was decorated in different ways, if the wearer had the sufficient means. A simple shirt and skirt-like wrap-around waistcloth could also be worn, but this is hard to ascertain since reliefs invariably show belts being worn, so the differences between full-length tunics and the latter combination are difficult to make out.

Murals and bas-reliefs depict various garments being worn according to social rank and ethnic background. The king and his dignitaries wore a large shawl draped around the body in various ways. Depending on the wearer's rank, it would have been richly embroidered and decorated with fringes, coloured borders, and tufts. Ordinary Assyrians wore tunics of different lengths, most ending above the knees. Some wore various forms of legwear. Vassals, mercenaries and allies seem to have stuck to their own distinctive national dress. Reliefs show auxiliaries (mostly archers) clad in short waistcloths leaving the upper body bare. These troops seem to be soldiers recruited from among the Aramean tribes living in southern Mesopotamia, whose native costume was richly patterned and embroidered.

Clothing was influenced by local climate, season, and geographic circumstances. Although the sources ignore this aspect, campaigns in colder regions must have necessitated the wearing of clothes which covered the arms and legs and generally warded off the effects of cold climate. To keep warm, Assyrian soldiers will have worn cloaks or long-sleeved tunics when fighting in the mountains or northern provinces. These garments were surely made of wool, and cloaks may have been lined with fur. Pictorial sources are lacking however. Breeches and leggings became popular during Sargon II's reign and were probably adopted from the mounted people of the steppes. Breeches and leggings came in various lengths, and according to fragments of coloured bas-reliefs, were often striped in contrasting colours. It is not entirely clear how close-fitting these forms of legwear actually were. Depending on the fabric and the individual wearer, these garments were probably not always quite as sleek as the reliefs imply.

Like modern footwear, Assyrian boots sported a tongue flap and laces bound crosswise[62]. Beginning at the foot, the bootstraps were laced upwards to the bottom of the knee, and then wound around the leg and tied up. This method of tying the boot also provided a kind of garter and so helped to keep the trousers or leggings in place. Assyrian reliefs show soldiers walking barefoot or wearing sandals, shoes, or boots. It is hard to conceive that on campaign against mountain peoples like the Urarteans, Assyrian soldiers would have done without some form of footwear, and fought only clad in skimpy, short-sleeved tunics. Of course, light clothing would have been the obvious choice when on campaign in the Syrian and Arabian desert, or when fighting in Egypt or the Sea Country along the Persian Gulf.

61 The translation is possibly inaccurate. It appears that the king is referring to red wool and birds whose feathers had been dyed.

62 Boots were not an Assyrian invention. Hittites, Urarteans, and the mounted nomads of the northeast, the Manneans and Medes, wore them. Bas-reliefs depicting the delivery of annual tributes show men (probably Medes or Manneans) wearing boots or laced gaiters, some of which extend to above the knee. It is unclear how far this footwear reached, as tunic hems obscure the tops.

MILITARY EQUIPMENT

Surviving original contemporary artefacts from the Sargonid era are very rare. Only few finds from 2,500 years ago have thus found their way into museums or private collections. Of Assyrian leatherwork or textiles there exists not even fragmentary archaeological evidence. Only a handful of metal objects employed either in an economic or miltary context have been found. Since bronze is less perishable than iron and low-quality steel and iron corrode easily, most finds are bronze. It was also fairly common to melt down disused iron objects and reforge them into artefacts more urgently needed. This practice can be explained with the high economic significance iron possessed.[63] Although more bronze artefacts have survived than iron, it would be misleading to draw conclusions regarding the respective frequency with which both materials were employed during the Sargonid era. The transition between the bronze and iron ages had after all long since occurred. Assyria possessed neither rich natural resources of iron ore nor other metals and was thus forced to rely on trade, tributes and spoils to cover its demand. Copper was imported from Cyprus and Anatolia, while tin was purchased from the Phoenicians via the East and northern Syria. Although some iron ore could be obtained in Assyria itself, Urartu provided pure iron in large quantites. Assyria exclusively made use of pure tin-bronze alloys, since the quality-enhancing addition of zinc was as yet unknown, and zinc resources would have been scant at any rate. Any zinc contents in Assyrian bronze alloys are therefore entirely coincedental. With a high copper content, Assyrian bronze artefacts possess a distinctly reddish colour and lack the golden tinge common to Roman helmets, since the higher proportion of zinc responsible is missing. The average metal proportion in Mesopotamian bronze alloys is 8 to 12% tin, and 87 to 91% copper. Other metals such as lead formed ca. 1%. Iron and bronze were used alongside each other and were of equally high importance. Both metals could not be welded together due to their respective material qualities, so had to be joined mechanically. In the case of military or domestic objects this mostly occurred by riveting. A fragment of an Assyrian pointed helmet has survived, whose bowl originally consisted of one bronze and one iron half. Both were joined with the help of rivets passing through a raised comb running from front to back. The bipartite comb was formed by two flanges. The prolonged use of bronze objects in the entire Assyrian era can be explained by its high degree of durability, its limited quantity, and the resulting economic value.

Since the few surviving original objects of the Assyrian military trade are exclusively of metal, we are forced to look to pictorial sources for further information on Assyrian military equipment. Some of these sources are open to a wide range of interpretation. Assyrian warriors are shown wearing helmets, headbands, diadems and bonnets. Some of these were of metal, others consisted of leather or fabrics. Metal headwear was lined with leather or fabric for comfort and to protect it from perspiration. The Assyrian royal headdress, the distinctive *tiara*, naturally deserves pride of place. It normally consisted of a textile base, to which bronze or golden hoops were attached. The *tiara* was not worn in combat. Since Assyrian monarchs habitually commanded in person, they went to war wearing high-quality protective equipment. A relief at Nineveh discovered by Layard shows episodes from the campaign against the Elamites. The Assyrian commander wears a pointed helmet. The relief is from the time of Ashurbanipal however, who did not always take the field in person. In his account of the battle of Halule[64] fought in 691 BC, Sennacherib writes that he donned a corselet and helmet before going into action. Reliefs mostly show the king wearing the *tiara*, but this was artistic convention and done to make the king instantly recognizable. The standing army and professional mercenaries will have worn durable military equipment of high quality. Provincial levies and foreign auxiliaries wore everyday civilian garb supplemented by body armour, if available. Peasants who were conscripted into the Assyrian army would draw their equipment from the arsenals provided by the government.

---

63   It is fairly certain that disused military equipment was used for civilian purposes or melted down and reforged into new, more modern military equipment.

64   His account is inscribed on the Taylor prism.

Previous double spread:

Assyrian infantry and dog handler

Warrior with spear and crested helmet

The warrior in the foreground wears a crested helmet as depicted in similar form on Assyrian reliefs. The helmet has been reconstructed according to an original find on offer at Gorny und Mosch auctioneers in 2016. It is not clear whether this helmet is of Assyrian, Urartean or Syrian origin. However, it is quite plausible that it was either worn by a mercenary in Assyrian service or acquired as booty by an Assyrian regular. The helmet's various sheet metal components were riveted together. The soldier also wears a large decorated circular chestplate made of bronze. Such items of armour came in various sizes. While small and medium examples seem to have been fairly common according to the sources, larger ones are comparatively rarely depicted but will no doubt have been just as frequently worn. The embossed decorations have been reconstructed according to original bronze finds. The broad sash-like belt decorated with bronze plates and the bowcase follow depictions on bas-reliefs. The bronze circular shield is based on a find now in the collection of the Christoph Bacher Archäologie Ancient Art Galerie in Vienna, Austria. It was probably excavated in Luristan. This shield type is frequently shown on Assyrian reliefs and was widely used by Assyrian troops. The figure's entire equipment suggests a fairly wealthy and experienced professional soldier. The veteran's elaborate and well-groomed beard follows depictions of facial hair on Assyrian reliefs. These depictions idealized the troops' appearance however, and on campaign a more rag-tag and scruffy appearance would have been likely. Assyrian sculptors followed artistic conventions and made use of different hairstyles and beards to distinguish between different ethnic groups.

Warrior with spear and pointed helmet

This soldier wears an iron helmet lacking earpieces. Helmets of this type are fairly frequent finds. A bronze example can be found in the collection of the Manchester Museum. Two wire loops are still attached to the sides to accommodate a chin strap or to attach cheekpieces. He carries a wickerwork shield and an iron scale corselet. His primary weapon is a heavy spear, supplemented by a sword. Reliefs frequently show warriors without sidearms. The leather backing of his corselet has been dyed, although evidence for such practice is lacking.

Dog handler

Dogs are often depicted in ancient Mesopotamian hunting scenes. Mostly however they were employed as sheep or cattle dogs, and guarded homesteads. They may occasionally have been used to hunt down human quarry, but it is far from certain if they were actually employed in combat. The dogs depicted on the bas-reliefs are very probably Mastiffs or belong to a related ancestral breed. The dog handler wears a headband popular with Assyrians and neighbouring peoples alike. He wears a tunic and sandals but does without legwear. His armament consists of a sword worn on a baldric.

ASSYRIAN ARMS AND ARMOUR

Helmets

Archaeological finds and reliefs have shown that the Assyrian army of the Sargonids made use of at least seven types of helmet. Round helmets, pointed helmets, conical helmets, conical helmets with cut-out browband, crested and ridged helmets were all worn.[65] True comb helmets did not exist as yet during the Sargonid period – archaeological evidence is lacking at any rate. It is possible however that comb helmets acquired as booty were worn by Assyrian troops.

All seven main Assyrian helmet types exist in various sub-categories. Variants can be distinguished according to manufacture (bronze, iron, and leather), and appearance. Helmets come in different sizes and shapes, some include protection for the ears, cheeks or neck while others are of simpler design. Ear- or cheekpieces were either strapped, studded or hinged to the helmet bowl, or formed integral parts of the helmet bowl itself. Crested and ridged helmets could differ in the types of crest attached. Crests were mostly manufactured of two metal halves enclosing a tuft or comb of horse or goat hair. This comb was probably dyed in similar manner as later Greek and Roman helmet crests were. Sometimes probably entire horse tails were used for individual helmets, whereas other crests would have been entirely of metal.

Several museums and private collections possess examples of Urartean and Assyrian pointed or crested helmets. Bronze and iron helmets of various forms consist of chased sheet metal up to 1,5 mm in strength. Many have several embossed bands running around the base of the bowl to increase stability. Some examples are up to 3 mm thick at the rim. In spite of this stout manufacture, the overal weight of Assyrian bronze helmets does not normally exceed 1 kg. Assyrian pointed helmets are 265 to 310 mm in height on average, and 190 to 225 mm in diameter at the base. Assyrian artists were careful to show the elaborate manufacture of the soldiers' helmets on triumphal reliefs. Helmets were used as long as they were serviceable. In times of peace they were stored in the various government arsenals. Storage often led to corrosion, but helmets also became discoloured or corroded by other influences, for instance rain, soot or perspiration. The soldiers will have polished their helmets frequently, causing the prominent parts of embossed decorations and ridges to gradually become brighter than the less accessible grooves and furrows. Bronze helmets were more susceptible to this phenomenon. While prominent flutings and ornaments would have shone brightly, dark green or black patina gathered in the helmets' various grooves and recesses.

The British Museum houses one slightly damaged Assyrian iron helmet and several fragments of others. All were found at Nimrud and can be dated to the Sargonid era. The helmets also possess bronze components. Attempts at reconstruction have shown that iron helmets frequently had bronze hoops or rings running around the bowl. Some had bronze plates with religious motives riveted on. Such magnificent helmets were probably worn by officers and guardsmen, or used for ceremonial purposes. The only more or less complete iron helmet in the British Museum's collection weighs ca. 3 kg. All other helmet finds, all of them made of bronze (which has a higher specific weight than iron), weigh less than 1,5 kg. The iron helmet is thus untypically heavy and will not have been worn in combat. The standard helmet type most easy to produce consisted of two half-bowls of bronze and iron respectively, which were riveted together creating a pronounced ridge running from front to back. Simpler types were hammered out of a single piece of sheet iron or bronze. Most surviving examples are made of bronze, so it is hard to assess how many Assyrian helmets were made of bronze, and how many of iron, or both. It is highly probable that most helmets worn by soldiers of the Neo-Assyrian army were made of iron, many of them sporting bronze decorative elements such as rims, studs, or embossed plates. Bas-reliefs depict the Assyrian soldier in his most resplendent turnout. If the king himself makes an appearance, it is his guardsmen who wear the most elaborate equipment.

All helmets possessed leather or fabric linings, or were worn over some other form of padding, e. g. a cap or head-band. Surviving helmets have holes punched along the rim of the bowl to accommodate the stitching for the lining. Wearing the helmet without padding would have resulted in extreme discomfort and serious injury in the case of a blow to the head. Some helmet finds have traces of asphalt adhering to the inside of the bowl. It is unclear whether this asphalt was a leftover from the manufacturing process or served as an adhesive substance for the lining. Chinstraps were worn to keep the helmet in place. These were either attached to the side of the bowl, or to the cheekpieces. Some cheekpieces seem to have been made of organic materials, e. g. leather.

Reliefs show Assyrian soldiers and their enemies and allies not only wearing helmets but all sorts of different protective headgear, e. g. bonnets, headbands and diadems. Exactly what materials they were made of is difficult to determine from a modern point of view. If it were to possess some protective function against enemy weapons, such headgear would have had to be made of bronze, iron, or leather. However, many probably made do with simple cloth headbands.

---

65 Some scholars claim that none of these helmet types were genuine Assyrian inventions.

Assyrian crested helmet

Bronze, chased and embossed, ornaments riveted on, front view.

Height: 28, 5 cm, diameter: 28, 5 cm; weight: 790 g.

Badisches Landesmuseum Karlsruhe.
Photograph by Peter Gaul

Organic components (horsehair crest and and lining) are missing. The helmet's age is hard to assess. Expert opinions vary greatly, claiming manufacture between 860 and 727 BC. The helmet was probably used much longer at any rate. The engraved religious image points to Assyrian origin.

Assyrian crested helmet
Bronze, chased and embossed, ornaments riveted on, side view.
Photograph by Peter Gaul

Warrior wearing crested helmet
Paul-Émile Botta, *Monument de Ninive*, vol. 2, plate 117 (S. 69).
Digital library, University of Heidelberg.

The warrior on the right wears a crested helmet, while the soldier on the left is equipped with a ridged helmet. The Assyrians are employing battering rams to breach the walls of the besieged city.

Assyrian warriors wearing round helmets

Austen Henry Layard, *The Monuments of Nineveh*, plate 94 (page 123).
Digital library, University of Heidelberg.

Depictions of this helmet type are rare. It was however in widespread use in the Middle East during the Sargonid era.

Assyrian bronze crested helmet

Gorny & Mosch Giessener Münzhandlung GmbH München, Auktionshaus. Photograph by Michel Girschick, Starnberg.
Height: 40cm; diameter: 22cm; ca. 9th-8th century BC

The helmet was registered as Assyrian or Urartean by the auctioneers. This is impossible to determine exactly, both origins are entirely possible. Many reliefs show this helmet type as forming part of Assyrian military equipment. The helmet is composed of two chased halves which have been riveted together to form the bowl. The cheekguards have also been riveted on. The bowl is conical and features two horizontal bands, one towards the apex, the other runnning around the base. The tapering crest holder is drawn down low towards the front of the helmet. The cheekguards are cut out at eye and mouth level similar to later Celtic and Roman helmets. All rims and edges feature holes to accommodate the stitching of lining and crest.

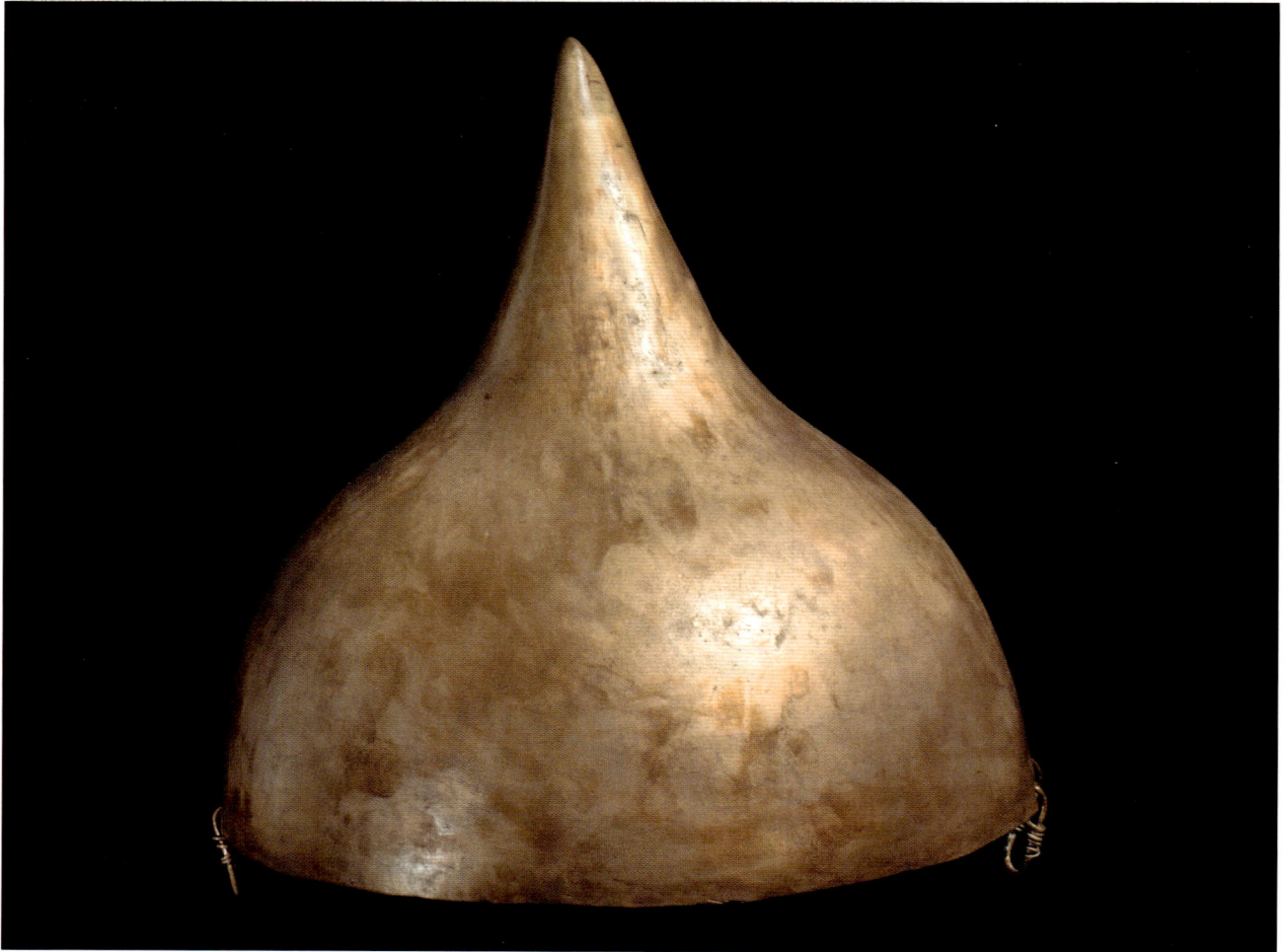

Assyrian bronze helmet
Manchester Museum, 7th-8th century BC.
Height: 21 cm; diameter: 19,7 cm; weight: not specified.
Information courtesy of Dr. Campbell-Price, Manchester Museum.

This simple and fairly shallow pointed helmet was excavated at Thebes and probably found its way to Egypt during the 25th Egyptian dynasty (Kushite dynasty). Referred to by the Manchester Museum as a helmet of Syrian type, it is probably of Assyrian manufacture. The rings attached to the side of the helmet accomodated the leather chinstrap.

Right:
Assyrian warriors wearing low pointed helmets of the type shown above.
Paul-Émile Botta, *Monument de Ninive*, vol. 1, plate 62 (page 70).
Digital library, University of Heidelberg.

The bas-relief shows three warriors equipped with pointed helmets. It is one of the few reliefs whose colours have survived partly intact.

Assyrian bronze pointed helmet

Hermann Historica München, Internationales Auktionshaus für Antiken, Alte Waffen, Orden und Ehrenzeichen, Historische Sammlungsstücke

This find is similar to the Manchester helmet. It is a standard piece of Assyrian equipment often depicted on Assyrian reliefs.

Assyrian (Babylonian?) bronze pointed helmet

Front view   Rear view

Christoph Bacher Archäologie Ancient Art Wien, www.cb-gallery.com
Height: 38,5 cm. 8th-7th century BC.

This helmet is in virtually perfect condition. It is of conical shape and including the cheekpieces was manufactured from a single sheet of bronze. The helmet bowl curves slightly outward and culminates in a high peak. The rim of the bowl has been punctured with holes set in pairs to permit the attachment of a lining, which probably also ran along the helmet's outer edge.

The overlapping edges of the original sheet were fastened at the back of the bowl by four metal staples, three of which have survived in place. The helmet originated in the northern provinces of the Neo-Assyrian empire and probably belonged to an Assyrian or Babylonian warrior. Again, this is a fine specimen of Assyrian standard military equipment.

Assyrian bronze pointed helmet

Vorderasiatisches Museum, Staatliche Museen Berlin. Photograph by Olaf M. Teßmer

Height: 37, 7 cm; diameter: 22 cm; weight: 1460 g. 9th-7th century BC. Excavated at Zinjirli

A standard piece of military equipment judging by depictions on Assyrian reliefs. The lower rim has several bands embossed for increased stability and strength. This helmet lacks the customary holes around the rim. The lining was probably glued to the inside.

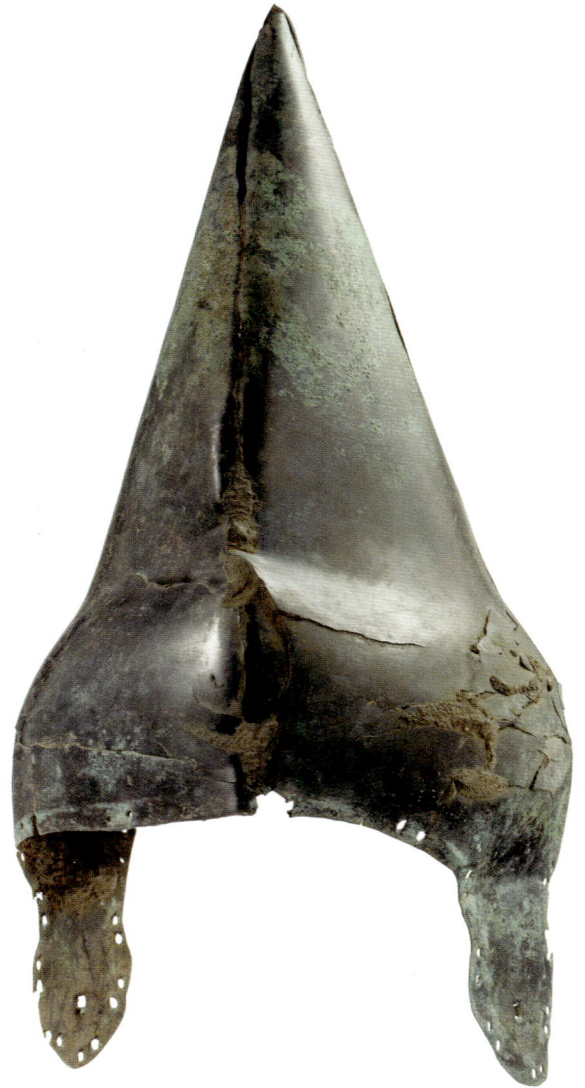

Assyrian bronze pointed helmet

Front view   Rear view

Hermann Historica München, Internationales Auktionshaus für Antiken, Alte Waffen, Orden und Ehrenzeichen, Historische Sammlungsstücke.

Height: 43 cm; weight: 602 g. 8th-7th century BC.

Standard Assyrian helmet with integrated cheekguards. The holes for lining and chinstrap are clearly visible. The helmet was manufactured from one sheet of bronze and stapled at the rear.

Decorated bronze helmet

Museum zu Allerheiligen, Schaffhausen (CH). Photograph by Ivan Ivic.

Height: 30,9 cm; diameter: 23 cm; weight: 710,9 g. 8th-7th century BC.

This magnificently engraved and embossed piece of equipment is a true masterpiece of Assyrian craftsmanship and probably belonged to an officer. The embossed ridge running down the middle of the helmet terminates in a protome in the shape of a lion's head. The arches forming the edges of the browband may depict snakes with rams' heads. The engraved browband shows a religious scene. Some scholars believe the helmet to be Urartean. The figures' dress, the mythical characters, and the winged sun above the tree of life all point to Assyrian origin however. All of these depictions can also be found on a bas-relief at Khorsabad.

Assyrian foot spearman with crested helmet

The warrior wears a crested bronze helmet, a few fragments of which have survived and are now in the collection of the Badisches Landesmuseum at Karlsruhe, Germany. This type of helmet was at least as popular as the pointed helmet. Some examples were probably made of iron. The crest itself was probably of horsehair. His body armour consists of a circular bronze chest protector, which is fastened with the help of crossed leather straps. These breastplates could also be made of iron. We do not know whether the warrior's back was protected by a matching plate. Many chestplates were decorated with embossed patterns or images. The warrior seeks to protect himself with a wicker shield, which lacks a leather covering. Some Assyrian shields were also made of bronze or wood. Some wooden and wickerwork shields were faced with bronze sheeting. Urartean bronze shields were also employed when available. The warrior's short tunic is decorated at the hem and sleeves. The patterns were either stitched or consisted of bronze applications. The soldier does without legwear and wears sandals. Some Assyrian warriors and auxiliaries even preferred to fight barefoot, temperatures permitting. The bracelet is possibly a military decoration.

Religious image

Austen Henry Layard, *The Monuments of Nineveh*, plate 7 (page 35).

Digital library, University of Heidelberg.

The image strongly resembles the embossed motive on the Schaffhausen helmet's browband (see p 109).

Assyrian warriors wearing crested helmets besiege a city

Paul-Émile Botta, *Monuments de Ninive*, vol. 1, plate 68 (page 77).
Digital library, University of Heidelberg.

The two warriors in the foreground are equipped with crested helmets, circular breastplates, spears, swords, and round wicker shields. Several Assyrian soldiers are attempting to fire the gates of the besieged town. Their shields are probably bronze and thus more suitable for this perilous job.

Relief from the palace of Sargon II at Khorsabad

Paul-Émile Botta, *Monument de Ninive*, vol. 1, plate 63 (page 71).
Digital library, University of Heidelberg.

The warrior on the right wears a pointed helmet and is armed with bow and lance. The structure of his round shield suggests bronze manufacture. The shield possesses a hand grip and a fastening for the forearm (obscured here) probably similar to later hoplite shields. The soldier serves as an escort to the royal chariot. Sargon II rides in triumph as the stripped and mutilated corpses of his defeated enemies lie below.

Swords

Swords most commonly used in the Assyrian army were either short stabbing swords or long swords. The Mesopotamian sickle-bladed sword, which was also very popular in Egypt, had largely fallen out of use by the Sargonid era. It is frequently hard to clearly distinguish between daggers, short and long swords[66], and the transitions between the various categories are fuzzy at best. An Assyrian short sword measured between 51 and 71 cm, long swords consequently measure more than 71 cm. A bronze sword from the Middle Babylonian era recently on sale from an antique dealer measured 67,7 cm in length and 5,05 cm in width. Pictorial sources depicting the use of swords in Assyrian warfare are extremely rare. Even when cutting off heads, Assyrian soldiers seem to have relied on their daggers. For material reasons, Assyrian swords were used solely for stabbing. A coloured mural from Til Barsip shows an Assyrian warrior dispatching an enemy with either a curved sword or a large dagger. These images were created before the Sargonid era however.

66 Definitions vary according to the era concerned and scholars' individual tastes. For example, the blade of a Roman *gladius*, epitome of the ancient short sword, measured 60 cm.

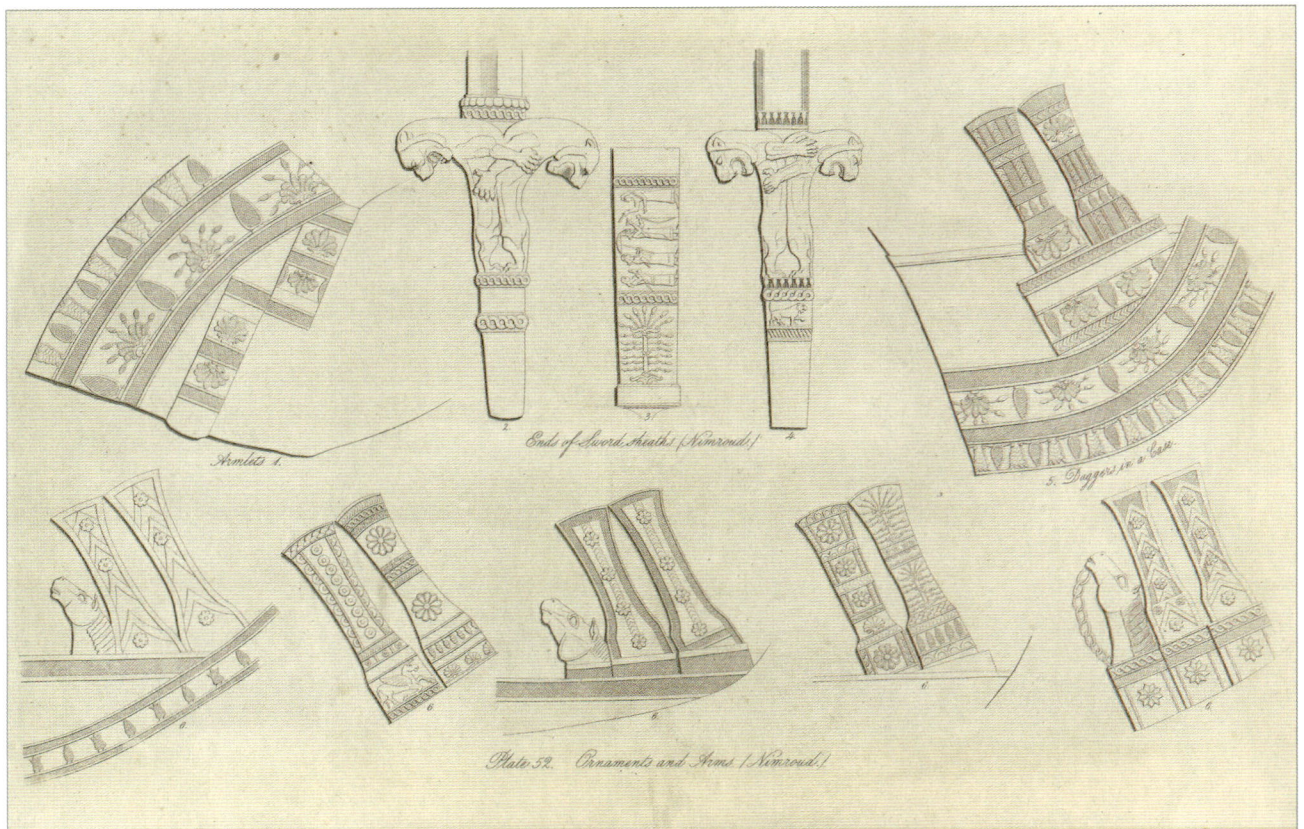

Details of Assyrian sword grips from various sources
Austen Henry Layard, *The Monuments of Nineveh*, plate 52 (page 81).
Digital library, University of Heidelberg.

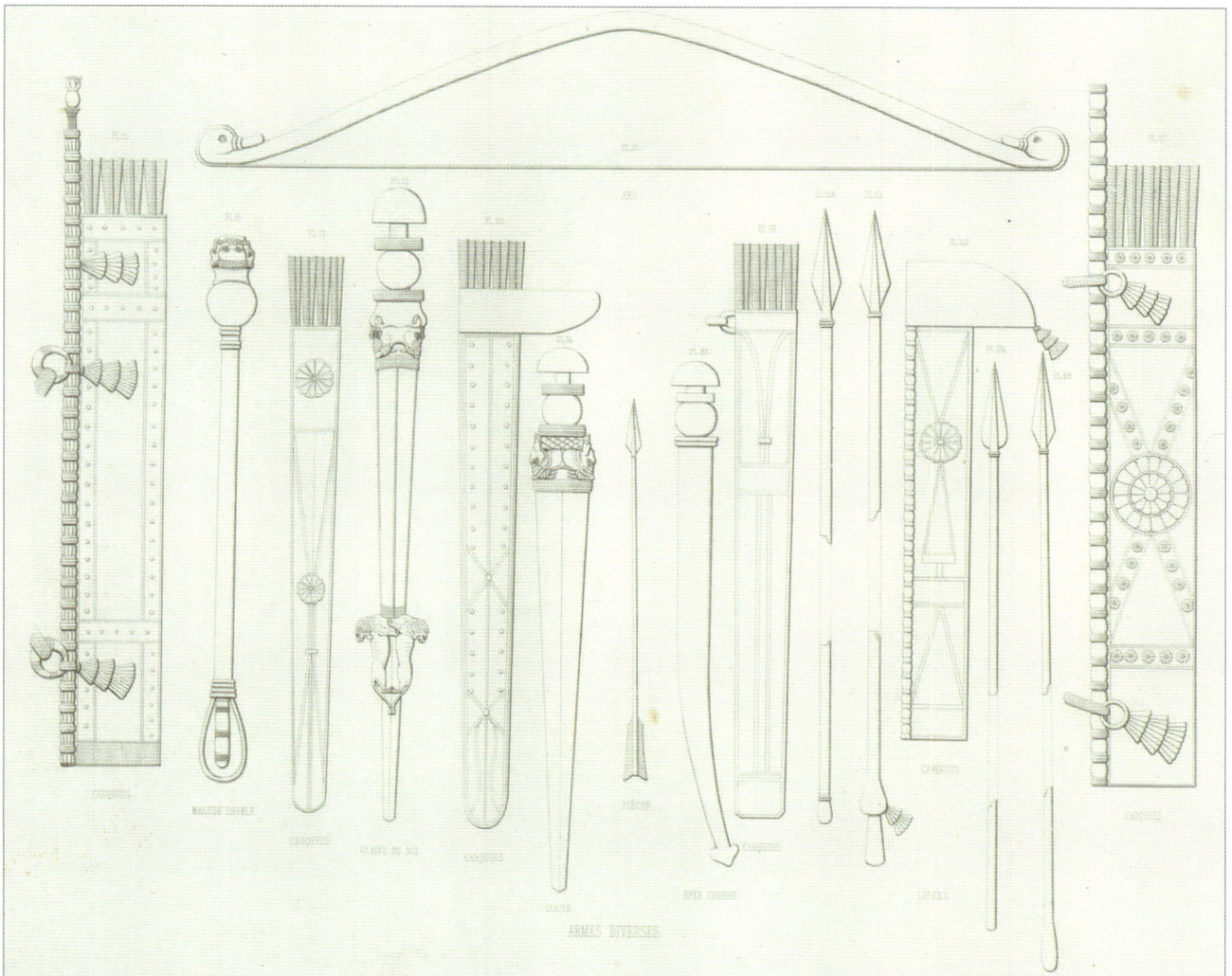

Assyrian arms

From various reliefs at Khorsabad. Paul-Émile Botta, *Monument de Ninive*, vol. 2, plate 159 (S. 82), Digital library, University of Heidelberg.

Collage of various depictions at Khorsabad. The artist has adopted the proportional inaccuracies of the Assyrian sculptors. The sword and dagger grips are in all probability incorrectly rendered for ergonomic reasons.

Hatchets, axes and maces

Other arms included hatchets wielded with one hand, and two-handed axes. Some axes had double heads. Reliefs frequently show Assyrian warriors holding maces with round heads. Such weapons were supplemeted by rods and batons, and may have been a sign of rank denoting officers and guardsmen, but this is far from certain. Some bas-reliefs showing Sennacherib's siege of Lachish feature Assyrian warriors carrying short sticks. These too might have served to identify officers.

Daggers and knives

Many warriors were armed with a single-edged knife or a double-edged dagger, which might measure up to 50 cm.

Bows

The main weapon of the ancient Near and Middle Eastern Warrior was the bow. Bows differed in material, and construction. There were both simple and recurved variants. Simple straight bows existed alongside angular and D-shaped models.[67] Preceded by simple wooden canes strengthened by sinew or rope bindings, the powerful composite bow began to evolve in Mesopotamia from the 17th century BC onwards. Its manufacture was lengthy and complicated, yet its performance was unmatched. A composite bow took at least a year to make due to the process of glueing together different materials to achieve the weapon's flexibility. Glues were made of natural substances, and experts believe that a high-quality composite bow would even have taken up to two years to manufacture. The bow's belly was reinforced with plates of horn while strips of animal sinew were glued to the the back (the bow's core, i. e. the riser and the limbs, was made of wood). All these different materials were assembled and then wound about with bast fibre and glued using natural resins.

The bow's singular power resulted from the combination of forces created by the compressed horn plates and the stretching of the sinew components. It is unclear how high the proportion of composite bows in use was in any Assyrian army (or any other, at that) during the era under examination. Princes and generals, chariot crews and élite troops will have been equipped with these elaborate and expensive weapons. In contrast to simpler examples, composite bows did not normally lose their elasticity and tension if they remained strung for longer periods of time. However, due to the glues employed in its manufacture, composite bows were extremely susceptible to disintegrating under damp conditions and could therefore only be used in dry weather. To protect such bows from the elements, archers carried their weapons in leather bow-cases, many examples of which can be seen in Median, Scythian and Assyrian art. The Old Testament records the use of simple bowcases during the reign of King David. Bows were unstrung on the march and in camp, and when no action was likely. Stringing a composite bow was hard physical exercise and depending on the bow's power might require up to two men. This was especially true for reflex bows, which had originally derived from the composite model. In unstrung condition, the bow limbs of these weapons actually point away from the archer. This bow type was probably introduced to Mesopotamia by the Scythians. The Assyrians may have acquired a small number of these bows as spoils or tributes from vassal princes. Reliefs certainly do not show them in Assyrian hands. The simple stave bows which were mainly used measured ca. 1,2 to 1,8 metres. Effective range did not exceed 80 to 120 metres. Composite bows were much shorter, measuring about 1,2 to 1,4 metres with effective range covering 160 to 175 metres. Arrows loosed from composite bows had twice as much penetrative power as arrows fired from ordinary bows. The shooting angle on the open battlefield was ca. 45°.

Arrows too underwent development. Arrowheads varied in design according to purpose, from stout armour-piercing heads to light and slender heads intended for long-range fire. It is highly probable that archers carried several types of arrow in their quivers to be employed according to the tactical situation at hand. Early arrowheads consisted of hardwood, flint or bone, but these were eventually phased out and replaced by arrowheads made of copper, bronze, and iron. During the Sargonid era, only bronze and iron arrowheads were used. Bronze arrowheads were cast, iron arrowheads forged. Shafts were likewise produced from different materials in order to achieve sturdiness and different flight characteristics. While shafts were usually made of straight and lightweight reed, both ends were reinforced with harder wood in order to improve balance and to provide the head with a sturdy mounting. The archer also needed a firm hold on the arrow when nocking it. To prevent the arrow splintering, it was usually wound with fibres immediately below the nock. Fletchings stabilized the arrow in flight. Arrows measured between 70 and 100 cm. A quiver could house up to 30 arrows. Quivers were made of wood, leather, or bronze, or from a combination of these materials. They were carried slung across the back. To protect the arrows (and the bow) from moisture, quivers and bowcases were equipped with a flap that covered the opening at the top and was folded back when the archer was using his weapon. Quivers were between 50 and 60 cm long. Archers wore bracers and leather finger tabs to protect hands and wrists while operating the bow. Bows manufactured solely of horn or iron were extremely rare. Metal arrows were employed as incendiary missiles. Bowstrings were made of waxed linen, animal gut, or sinew.

---

67   The limbs of angular bows are made so as to form a triangle together with the bowstring.

Assyrian archers stringing their bows

Relief from the Northern Palace at Niniveh. British Museum, London. Source: Wikipedia

In order to give arrows effective range and penetrative power, bows had to be capable of delivering the necessary kinetic energy. This meant that stringing the bow required considerable physical strength and skill, which could often enough only be provided by two men.

Bronze archery bracer

Hermann Historica München, Internationales Auktionshaus für Antiken, Alte Waffen, Orden und Ehrenzeichen, Historische Sammlungsstücke.

This Urartean bracer, of which front and rear views are given, is an example of the equipment worn by Middle Eastern archers to protect their wrists from the rebounding bowstring when the arrow was loosed. While many bracers would have consisted merely of a simple leather strap, others were more elaborate. In this case, a bronze plate was stitched to a leather backing. Assyrian reliefs frequently show archers with such equipment.

Slings

Due to its simplicity, the sling was the weapon of the common man. Its use was fairly easy to learn, and it had served shepherds for centuries when it came to protecting their flocks from wild animals. David the shepherd boy had felled Goliath with a well-aimed pebble from his sling. Slings were usually made from soft leather. Several slings of linen were found in Tutankhamun's grave in the Valley of Kings. Projectiles normally consisted of stones or pebbles. Range was up to ca. 300 metres. The sling itself consisted of a middle part which was a pocket-like receptacle for the stone, and two straps, one of which terminated in a loop into which the slinger slipped his index finger. He would let the other end go when the sling was released. The slinger would place a stone in the sling and whirl his weapon above his head several times, allowing the missile to gain momentum. The other strap was then released, and the sling propelled its missile towards the target.

Although unmentioned by the sources, slingers would have carried a satchel or bag with a number of projectiles. Due to the long range of their weapon, slingers will have formed the front ranks of the Assyrian line and opened the battle with a hail of deadly missiles.

Spears

There were more or less three basic types of polearms:
- ❏ Spears, which were about a man's length and wielded in one hand,
- ❏ Javelins, which were shorter and intended primarily for throwing,[68]
- ❏ Lances, which were longer than spears and wielded in both hands.

However, since some Assyrian reliefs show cavalrymen thrusting downwards with a long lance held in one hand only, this categorization can obviously not be regarded as a hard and fast rule. In close range combat, foot soldiers grasped spears in both hands to add power to their thrust. Since stirrups and saddles in the modern sense of the word did not yet exist, the problem of adding momentum to the use of the spear was felt especially among mounted troops. Excavated iron spearheads are between 13 and 30 cm in length. The spearhead was attached to the wooden shaft by various means, e. g. by a welded-on socket and bolt. Some lances had bronze butts. The Assyrians also employed javelins, which were generally shorter than spears. Throwing sticks do not seem to have been used as none have been found, and they are not depicted in Assyrian art.

Body armour

Assyrian bas-reliefs show several types of body armour, e. g. scale and lamellar corselets. Both types of armour were manufactured using scales or lamellae of bronze or iron. This is confirmed by archaeological finds. Scales came in many shapes and sizes, and the position of the holes punched in them in order to affix them to the backing also varied. The manner of attaching the scales to the leather or fabric backing differed according to the type of corselet produced: some scales or lamellae were attached so as to overlap each other horizontally as well as vertically, while others were not, instead forming parallel rows separated by leather stitching or panels. The question whether linen or leather corselets were worn is impossible to answer since they do not feature in the sources. It is however reasonable to assume that leather jerkins were worn by some warriors as a light and simple form of body protection.

We do not know whether the lamellar armour so popular with Assyrian sculptors was a genuine Assyrian invention. The Assyrian lamellar corselet differs from conventional scale armour in that the rows of scales were often interspersed with other materials (see above). It is believed that these were the different materials onto which the scales were mounted. This type of armour was especially favoured by charioteers, the crews manning the siege towers, and the sappers, but it could also be found among the foot soldiers and the cavalry.

Scale armour had been popular in the Middle East and Egypt for a long time. A scale corselet consisted of metal plates attached to an undergarment mostly of fabric or leather. The scales were sewn to the undergarment so that they overlapped both vertically and horizontally. This mode of manufacturing can be ascertained by a textile fragment with attached scales which was excavated at Thebes and made approximately during the reign of Amenhotep III (r. 1388–1351 BC). Since similar finds in an Assyrian context are lacking, scholars have attempted to reconstruct the appearance of Assyrian armour from various sources. In the case of scale armour this has proved remarkably successful.

Scale armour as described above no longer features on Sargonid reliefs, which does of course not mean that it was no longer worn. Scales dating from the Sargonid period were found at Nimrud, Sam'al, Ziyaret Tepe, and Lachish. Most of these finds can now be found in the collections of the British Museum, the Vorderasiatisches Museum in Berlin, the Royal Ontario Museum, and the Louvre. During the Neo-Assyrian period, especially under Tiglath-Pileser III, Assyrian soldiers were equipped with the latest type of body armour, the new lamellar cuirass. This type of corselet was more flexible thanks to the horizontal gaps between the rows of scales, and was cheaper to produce since the amount of metal required was smaller than with the conventional scale cuirass. It was also lighter and less cumbersome. Just how the various materials required

---

68   A skilled javelineer could use such weapons effectively within a range of between 20 and 30 metres.

were exactly combined in the corselet's production process remains to some extent guesswork. This is mostly due to the lack of organic materials in the relevant finds, and some scales are impossible to clearly assign to any specific form of armour. Attempts at reconstruction therefore reflect differing interpretations of the sources, and the archaeological material available.

Basically, lamellar armour consisted of a large number of scales (lamellae)[69] which were attached both to each other and the leather or textile backing. For this, pitched thread was employed. It is not clear whether the scales were attached to individual horizontal strips of leather which were sown together to form the corselet, or whether the backing consisted of a complete doublet. The decoded Assyrian term *siram* denotes a garment or leather doublet reinforced with metal plates, which would fit the bill nicely. Another likely interpretation would be a combination of leather strips and scales attached to a linen or leather undergarment.

Thus the Assyrian lamellar corselet probably did not consist only of a mass of scales simply joined together by lacing, as is in evidence for later periods.[70] The holes in the scales were simply too small to hold stouter laces which would have provided the higher degree of protection necessary to make this armour effective. If this type of armour did exist, it would have had to be worn over an additional garment. Climates with temperatures up to 41° C would have made wearing a corselet merely consisting of metal scales and lacking some form of padding a most unpleasant experience. In winter, temperatures in Assyria would frequently drop as low as −5° C. The areas in which Assyrian armies were expected to operate comprised a wide range of climatic conditions, reaching from the mountains of Urartu in the north to the Syrian and Arabian deserts, and Egypt and the Persian Gulf in the south. Thus the Assyrian soldier was forced to constantly modify and adjust his personal clothing and equipment to his surroundings. When reconstructing Assyrian armour the only reliable source apart from the archaeological finds is sculptural art in the form of the numerous reliefs excavated on Assyrian sites. However, these remain silent when it comes to determining the materials employed in the corselets' manufacturing. Assyrian scale and lamellar armour existed in very different variations regarding the size of the scales or lamellae, the scales' form (some incorporate a raised middle spine), the distance between individual rows of scales, the number of scales to a row, and the metal and backing material chosen by the manufacturer. Some cuirasses had short sleeves reaching to above the elbow rather like a modern t-shirt, while others covered only the upper torso. Some sleeves only seem to have been covered with scales either at the front or, curiously, at the back.Thus Assyrian scale or lamellar body armour could take a large variety of forms.

Another problem when turning to Assyrian bas-reliefs for information on body armour is the varying quality of their execution due to the individual style and skill of the sculptor concerned. We can deduce from sculptural evidence (although a certain amount of caution appears advisable) that stout linen was used in the manufacturing of body armour because Assyrian sculptors employed different techniques to make stone surfaces resemble or at least signify specific materials such as fabrics or parts of the soldiers' equipment. For example, the warriors' linen leggings, socks and breeches are generally adorned with a criss-cross, net-like pattern. The same pattern interestingly appears in the gaps between the rows of lamellar corselets. Presumably one of the fabrics employed in the production of lamellar cuirasses was linen.

This reduced the corselet's weight and increased the wearer's mobility, and facilitated ventilation. This was a vital aspect for soldiers who were expected to fight in hot climates without suffering sunstroke. Wedge-shaped patterns employed by sculptors seem to indicate leather as a backing for lamellar armour. Scales were sewn to the backing, the stitching passing through several holes punched into the scales. This method ensured that the scales remained immobile and thus maintained the corselet's protective quality.If the stitching became damaged at only one point, the scale would remain in place or at least not become completely detached. Even though Assyrian lamellar corselets left small gaps between the horizontal rows of scales, their protective value was nevertheless high. Several layers of leather or linen sewn together as explained above still provided a fairly high amount of protection against arrows, blunt trauma, or even spear thrusts. Linen corselets had already been worn by Egyptian troops several centuries before the period under examination. If the backing was to be made of leather, the armourers may have favoured cowhide.

Excavated scales are between 0,1 and 0,5 mm thick and of different size according to where they were attached. Sizes vary on average between 1,8 and 2,0 cm in breadth and 3,5 to 4,9 mm in length. Unimpeded movement of the wearer made scales of different sizes in the shoulder, upper arm, throat, chest, and belly regions a necessity. Scales in the throat and upper arm area were more slender than those around the chest. Scales came in semicircular, rectangular and droplet forms. The surviving scales have the holes required for attachment punched into them, and many have a central spine to improve stability. Since the specific weight of bronze is higher than that of iron, corselets were of different weights even if the number of scales was identical. The weight of Assyrian scale body armour has been calculated to amounting be-

---

69   A relief shows an archer and a shield bearer manning a siege tower, whose duty obviously is to cover the men operating the tower against the city's defenders.

70   Early mediaeval lamellar armour was produced by combining the rows of scales using broad leather straps so that these laces formed a thick layer of leather padding between the individual rows

Assyrian Warriors wearing lamellar armour
Paul-Émile Botta, *Monument de Ninive*, vol. 1, plate 49 (page 56).
Digital library, University of Heidelberg.

Iron scales from Zinjirli, 9th to 7th c. BC
Vorderasiatisches Museum,
Staatliche Museen Berlin.
Photograph Olaf M. Teßmer.

Excavations at Zincirli resulted in several finds of iron scales. Whether these formed part of either scale or lamellar armour is impossible to tell, since the fabric or leather backing has long since perished.

Assyrian warriors wearing lamellar armour
Paul Émile Botta, *Monument de Ninive*, vol. 2, plate 95 (page 15).
Digital library, University of Heidelberg.

Assyrian lamellar corselets differed in the shape, size, materials, positioning and strength of scales employed for manufacture. Since all armour was produced manually, many variants existed. The reliefs shown here, which were executed in great detail, were excavated at the palace of Sargon II at Khorsabad.

Assyrian warriors wearing lamellar armour

Paul Émile Botta, *Monument de Ninive*, vol. 1, plate 77 (page 86).
Digital library, University of Heidelberg.

tween 16 and 26 kilogrammes. Despite the susceptibility of iron to corrosion,a large number of iron scales have been found. It remeains unclear whether bronze or iron dominated the manufacturing of Assyrian scale armour. Often the corselets were provided with an apron of vertical leather straps at the bottom, which served to protect the wearer's thighs and groin.

Assyrian body armour further consisted of circular iron or bronze chest plates (peytrals) of varying size, which were secured by crossed straps. Some warriors will have worn similar plates to protect their backs. Bas-reliefs only show round chest plates, but a royal statue now in the collection of the New York Metropolitan Museum of Art wears what looks like a trapezoid chest protector. Thus we may conclude that this form of armour was not limited to circular form. A Scythian burial mound yielded fragments of a golden Iranian trapezoid chest protector.

Some reliefs show warriors wearing garments covered with rectangular patterns. This may depict jerkins or tunics to which small rectangular metal plates were attached. Such plates have been found in Urartean contexts. Compared to scale or lamellar armour this form of body protection must appear decidedly flimsy however, and there is reason to believe that the patterns discussed simply depict an elaborate form of textile pattern. Small decorated metal plates of various shapes and sizes have also been found on Assyrian sites. Scholars believe that such elaborate artefacts were in fact a form of decoration applied to the garments of high-ranking Assyrians.

Assyrian sources make a point of mentioning elephant hide as booty, or when it was delivered up as tribute. Since elephant hide is particularly thick, it may have been used in the manufacture of armour or belts, or possibly for footwear (soles), shield linings, or even protective headwear. Assyrian reliefs show comparatively broad belts, which may have been made of either textile or leather. Urartean finds make clear that these belts or sashes were frequently covered with strips of bronze, perhaps to protect the wearer's abdomen. Assyrian warriors are also often depicted wearing broad crossed leather shoulder belts. Since these also occasionally display patterns, they may likewise have been reinforced with metal plates or studs.

Horses wore fabric or leather bardings and metal peytrals for protection.The latter were mounted onto a leather backing. Several of these were often connected and strapped around a horse's neck resembling an elaborate necklace. Peytrals existed in various shapes and sizes and had been in use long before the Sargonid period. Some were presumably made entirely of leather. Elaborately decorated round bronze discs have been found on Urartean sites. Measuring between 25 and 30 cm in diameter, these have been interpreted as a decorative form of horse armour covering the animal's shoulder. Their protective quality was limited, and the same may be said of the chamfroms found in the same context, whose protective value was probably rather totemic than physical. Whether such shoulder plates and chamfroms were also employed by the Assyrians remains impossible to determine, but some Assyrian sources do at least suggest that they were. Assyrian reliefs show a peculiar form of head protection for horses, consisting of a beaded decorated headband of unknown manufacture (possibly padded) worn above the eyes. It is possible that this headdress was mounted on a leather backing and attached to the horse's head with straps of the same material. Horse headdress often resembled the crests worn on the helmets of the charioteers and cavalry troopers. It is only during the reign of Ashurbanipal that Assyrian pictorial sources begin to show horses with leather or cloth bardings. Especially the reliefs recording the campaign against Elam provide a lot of insight into this topic. Such bardings existed in a large variety of forms, often consisting of several different material components. This is especially true regarding the manner in which separate parts were connected, which parts of the body they covered, and how they were held in place.

City besieged by Assyrian troops

Austen Henry Layard, *A Second Series of The Monuments of Nineveh*, plate 39 (page 53).
Digital library, University of Heidelberg.

The relief from Nineveh shows Assyrians employing the man-high paveses especially popular with troops during sieges. They are similar in shape, but details vary. Obviously there was no standardized manufacturing method, and the shields were produced by individual craftsmen. Note the various flutings and grooves adorning the soldiers' helmets.

Shields

The Assyrian army employed a large variety of shields. Shields differed in both shape and size. Bas-reliefs show numerous examples, but unfortunately finds are rare. Those shields that have survived are exclusively of bronze manufacture. However, Assyrian shields were manufactured from a large number of different materials including wood, reed, leather, iron, and bronze. The cheapest and probably most frequently used shields were made of wickerwork. Especially for this purpose, reed was grown in river areas. A type of willow still common in northern Iraq was probably also used for the manufacturing of shields. The wicker shield surface was frequently covered with hide. In order to avoid damage to the edges and to maintain cohesion of the different components of their construction, shields were frequently lined with metal. Often a metal shield boss was attached, which helped support the central handgrip and protected the hand holding the shield. Shields were probably painted. Some shields made exclusively of metal had attached spikes, which allowed warriors to use their shields offensively and punch at their opponents with their shields at close quarters. Such shields no longer seem to have been in use during the Sargonid era however, since they no longer appear in contemporary Assyrian art. Bronze shields were decorated with embossed ridges and patterns to improve stabil-

ity. Archaeological finds include a bronze shield with an iron handgrip. The man-high paveses so often depicted in the context of sieges often feature a curved tip to provide additional protection for archers and engineers exposed to missiles from above. This type of shield was capable of providing cover for two men. Simple round shields measured ca. 60-80 cm in diameter and could be either flat or slightly conical. Some shields were rectangular in shape or had curved upper edges (this type is often referred to as the "Egyptian" variant). Curved tower shields would cover the entire man from chin to foot. The shield's curvature literally allowed the soldier to "step into" the shield and thus achieve a maximum amount of protection for the entire body. Shields were commonly held and carried with the aid of a central grip attached to the inside of the shield. On the march or during river crossings shields were frequently slung to the warrior's back with the aid of leather straps.

Complete panoplies including helmets, metal shields and body armour were extremely costly and were therefore mostly affordable only for mercenaries. Cuneiform inscriptions record that levies were provided with captured enemy armour or equipment from the royal arsenals. Clay tablets were issued as receipts when the men received equipment and destroyed once the equipment was returned.

Relief from the royal palace of Sargon II at Khorsabad

Musée du Louvre, Paris. Source: Wikipedia

The image shows three reliefs from different chambers in Sargon II's royal palace at Khorsabad. On the left, a genius provides divine blessing – a common motif in Assyrian art. The middle relief depicts two palace officials or courtiers, while on the right a soldier stands guard.

Relief from the royal palace of Sargon II at Khorsabad

University of Chicago Oriental Institute. Source: Wikipedia

A high-ranking dignitary followed by several court officials. The leading figure's elevated rank is shown by his elaborate beard and hairstyle, and his diadem. This type of headdress is frequently associated with the royal princes. The persons depicted are probably members of the royal entourage.

Assyrian warriors

Relief from the Northern Palace, Nineveh. British Museum, London. Source: Wikipedia

Two warriors are shown wearing a simple headband, tunics, leggings, and laced boots. They carry massive dished shields with round bosses and are probably guardsmen.

Assyrian warriors

Relief from the Northern Palace, Nineveh. British Museum, London. Source: Wikipedia

These warriors wear crested helmets with small cheek pieces and are equipped with curved so-called tower shields. They wear broad leather Urartean belts, which were probably decorated with bronze plating. They carry short swords as sidearms. All wear circular chest plates, but no shoes or sandals.

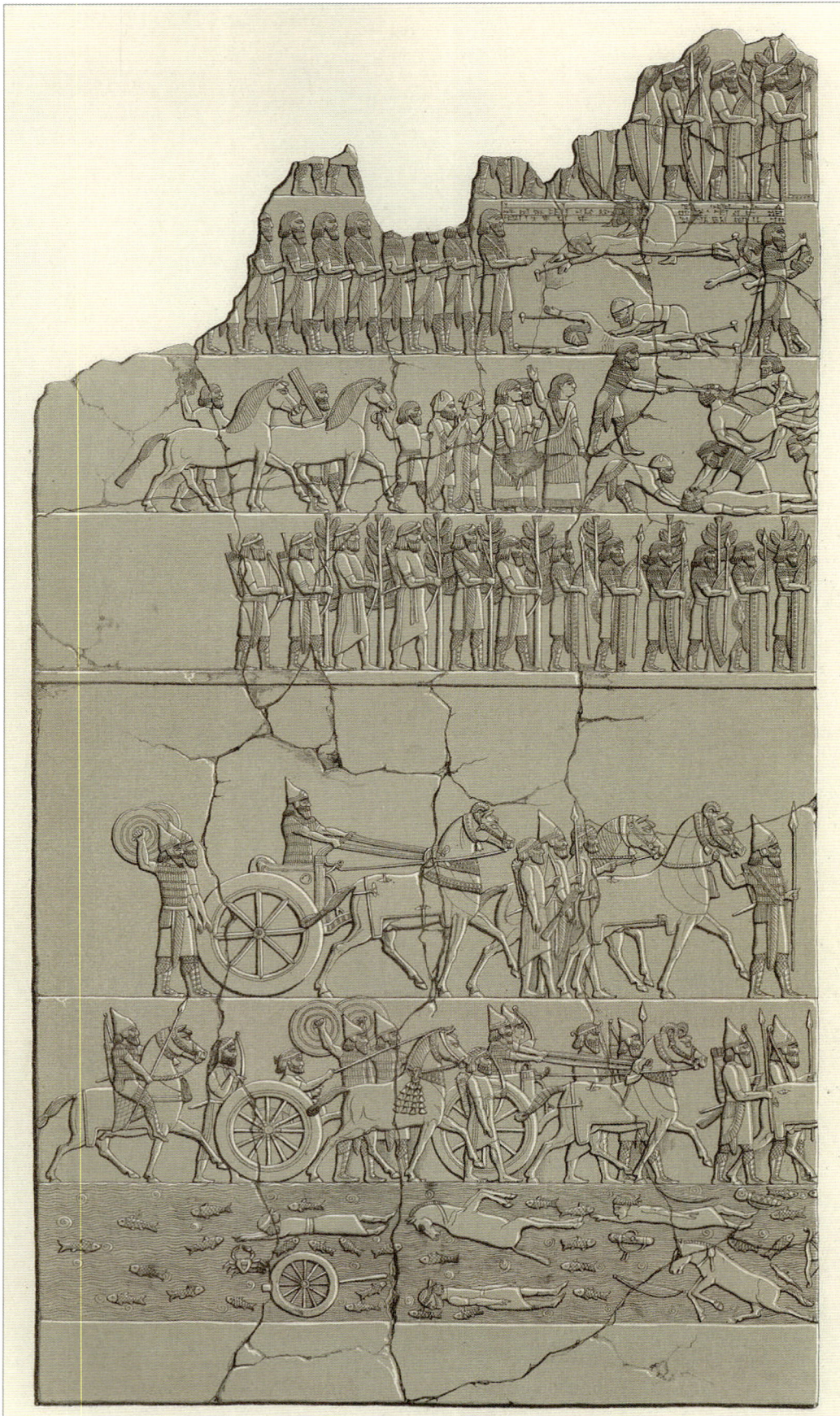

Assyrian troops equipped with different shield types

Austen Henry Layard, *A Second Series of The Monuments of Nineveh*, plate 47 (page 61). Digital library, University of Heidelberg.

Relief from the time of Ashurbanipal excavated at the Northern Palace, Nineveh.

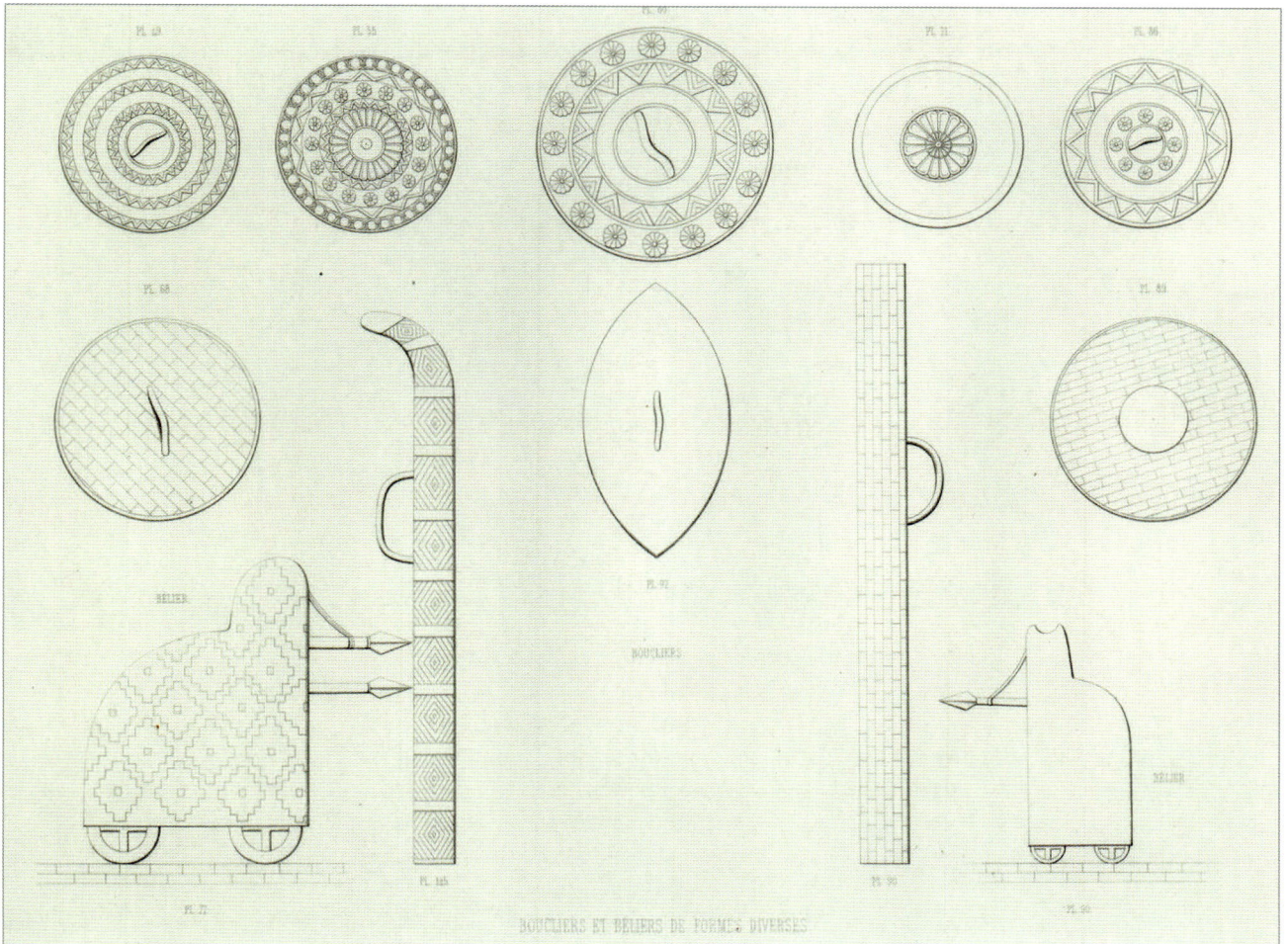

A compilation of various Assyrian shield types

Paul-Émile Botta, *Monument de Ninive*, vol. 2, plate 160 (page 83).
Digital library, University of Heidelberg.

From the reliefs at Khorsabad. Only a fraction of Assyrian shield types are depicted here.
Many more variations are known from other sources.

Assyrian chariot carrying religious standard
Paul-Émile Botta, *Monument de Ninive*, vol. 1, plate 57 (page 64).
Digital library, University of Heidelberg.

Relief from Khorsabad. Apart from housing a religious standard, the chariot also differs from others in that it has a religious symbol in the form of a semicircular disc mounted on the chariot pole above the yoke. This practice seems to have been a long-lived Assyrian tradition. The image is from the time of Sargon II.

THE STANDARDS

Pictorial sources do not show any standards in the conventional military sense. The two standards frequently shown mounted on chariots are depictions of the Assyrian deities Ninurta and Adad. These images were worshipped on campaign, temporarily replacing the effigies in the temples at home as objects of religious veneration. Assyrian warriors prayed and looked to them for divine protection and inspiration. Priests performed religious rites and sacrificed to them when the army was encamped. The standards consisted of religious images engraved or embossed on discs attached to long wooden or metal shafts. The discs themselves were made of gold or bronze, but wood also appears likely. When action was imminent, the standards were mounted on chariots so as to be visible to friend and for alike. How many of these the Assyrian army took on campaign is impossible to tell. Command chariots may have had them as part of their standard equipment. The standards themselves seem to have been supplemented by semicircular discs displaying religious symbols, which were mounted onto the chariot pole above the yoke.

Assyrian chariot carrying religious standard

Austen Henry Layard, *The Monuments of Nineveh*, plate 14 (page 43).
Digital library, University of Heidelberg.

This plate as well as the previous one both show Assyrian religious images displayed on war chariots in the form of military standards. While the previous image is from the reign of Sargon II, this one from the time of Ashurnasirpal, excavated at Nimrud, shows that the images did not change greatly over time.

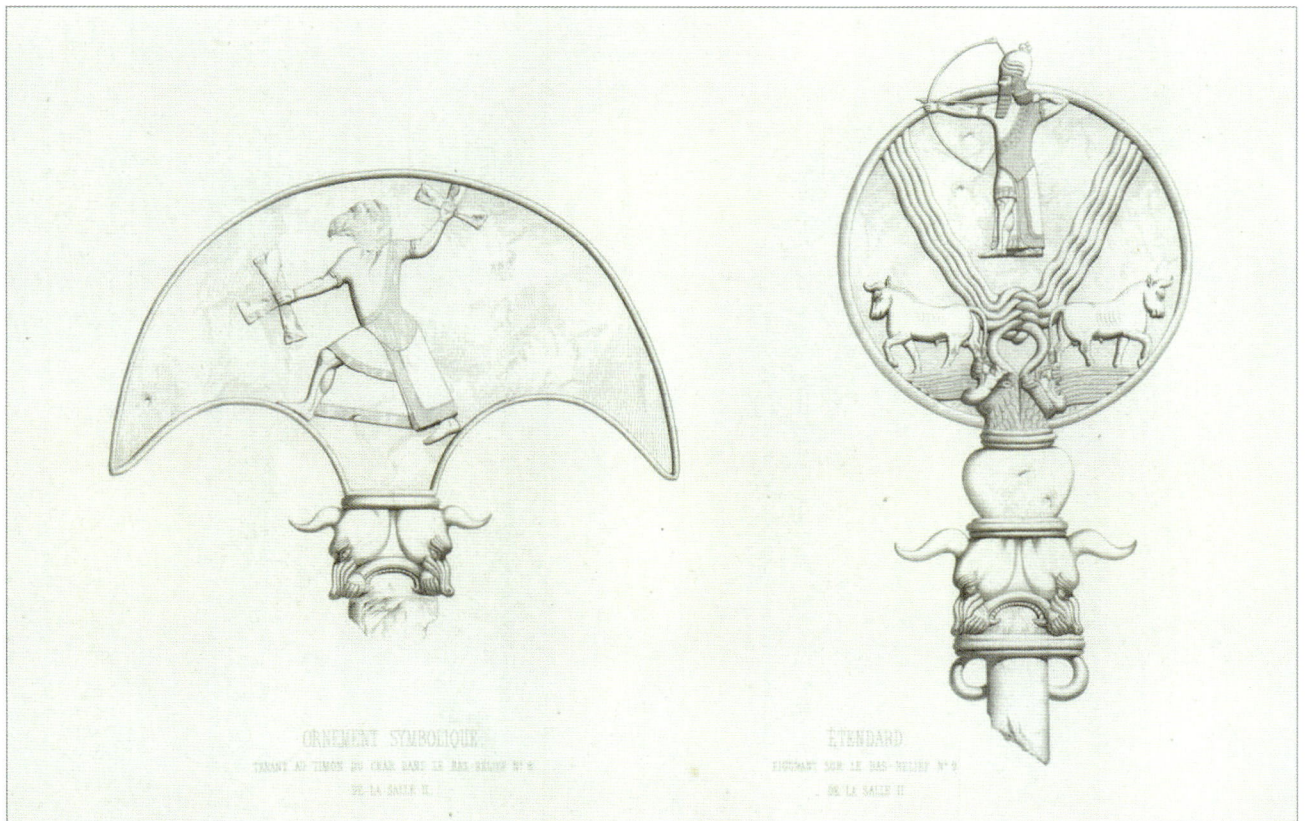

Assyrian religious standards

Paul-Émile Botta, *Monument de Ninive*, vol. 2, plate 158 (page 81).
Digital library, University of Heidelberg.

A detail of the Khorsabad reliefs, this plate shows standards from the time of Sargon II.

Previous double spread:

Officer with mace and trumpeter

The officer wears a bronze helmet formerly in the collection of Giancarlo Labue and currently in the collection of a Venice museum. Two very similar helmets formed part of the Axel Guttmann collection in Berlin but have since been sold. Decorated with embossed snakes and lions' heads, these helmets also sport religious images of Assyrian coronation or inauguration ceremonies on their browbands. Such helmets were definitely not standard issue. Similar helmets (some excavated in Luristan) are on display at the British Museum and the Badisches Landesmuseum at Karlsruhe, Germany. The helmet from the latter's collection is Urartean. All helmets have a high degree of similarity, which points to the extent of cross-cultural influence.

The body armour worn by both figures is based on archaeological finds of scales which have three double holes punched into them in order to attach them to a backing either of leather or strong fabric. The officer wears a corselet with five horizontal rows of scales, with scales also covering the outsides of the corselet's short sleeves. This is confirmed by Assyrian reliefs. He is armed with a bow and an iron sword, whose bronze grip and scabbard are both elaborately decorated. He also carries a mace as a further secondary weapon and sign of rank. He is bare-legged owing to the currently prevailing temperatures but wears the traditional Assyrian laced military boots, which were frequently worn in place of sandals. The coloured laces are conjectural but not unlikely. Reliefs still bearing traces of their original painting point to coloured footwear.

The trumpeter is similarly equipped. Layard depicts a relief showing a trumpeter attending the transportation of a stone relief (see next image). Assyrian trumpets differ slightly from instruments depicted in Egyptian art. Since no Assyrian instrument has been found, the above-mentioned relief is the only surviving source concerning Assyrian trumpets. His simple pointed helmet is based on an example now at the Manchester Museum. Both warriors wear earrings and bracelets, both of which are frequently depicted in Assyrian sculpture.

Assyrian trumpeters

Austen Henry Layard, *A Second Series of The Monuments of Nineveh*, plate 15 (page 29).
Digital library, University of Heidelberg.

Depictions of Assyrian trumpeters are very rare. Even though it depicts a civilian scene, this relief from Nineveh can also be used as a source for military trumpeters since the trumpet had already been in use by the military in Egypt for centuries. The trumpeters depicted are armed, which points to a military context. It is quite probable that other instruments besides the trumpet were used by the military, especially drums.

MILITARY MUSIC

Sources which concern themselves with Assyrian military music are scarce, yet some reliefs and inscriptions refer to its use, and which instruments were employed to make it. After the battle of Mount Uaush in 714 BC Sargon II returned to his camp in triumph, "...accompanied by the music of lyres, cymbals, and double flutes", as he proudly remarked.

Such instruments were however mostly played in a festive context. Reliefs depict harps, lyres, flutes, double flutes, cymbals, lutes, sistra, rattles, horns, trumpets, and various drums. To convey orders in battle, we may suppose that only instruments capable of carrying far such as trumpets, cymbals, horns, trumpets and kettle drums were used. A monumental relief now on display at the Vorderasiatisches Museum in Berlin shows several shield bearers and musicians carrying various instruments. Here, both the square frame drum and hand-held cymbals are in evidence for the first time in history. At the end of the triumphal procession walks a person identified either as a richly bejewelled woman or a beardless eunuch shouldering a round frame drum.

Sound signals to incite troops or to convey orders had been in use for centuries. The use of trumpets to convey messages is confirmed by an Assyrian relief depicting a civilian scene. It depicts the transportation of a large orthostat, the trumpets being employed to coordinate the actions of the numerous labourers responsible for moving it to its required position.

Of course an army in the field had to function just as smoothly as the complex procedures depicted on the relief. Advance and attack of different units or an entire force required precise synchronization and careful timing. Centuries before the Sargonid era, Egyptian armies made use of trumpets and drums on the battlefield. The report of an Egyptian drummer named Ehab has been dated to the period between 1648 and 1550 BC. Egyptian reliefs show trumpeters accompanying troops into battle. A Hittite relief excavated at Karkemish shows a man blowing a curved horn. The famous trumpets of Jericho of biblical fame may also hint at the use of wind instruments in a military context.

Assyrian musicians from the reign of Sennacherib

Vorderasiatisches Museum, Berlin.
Source: Wikimedia Commons

The musicians carry round and square frame drums and cymbals.

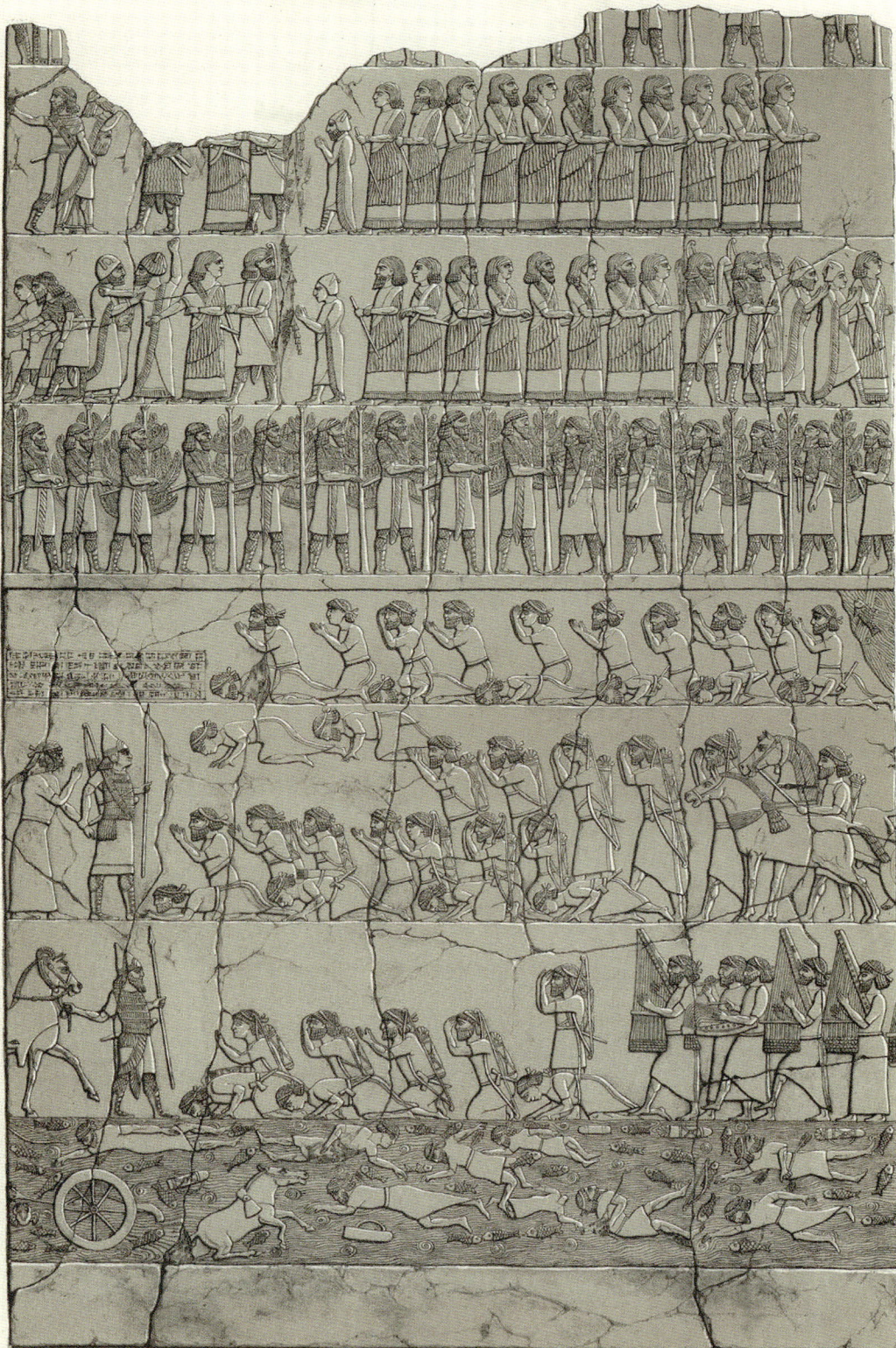

Elamite musicians
Austen Henry Layard, *A Second Series of The Monuments of Nineveh*, plate 28 (page 62).
Digital library, University of Heidelberg.

1

Musicians

Victor Place, *Ninive et l'Assyrie*, vol. 3, plate 59 (page 75).
Digital library, University of Heidelberg.

The reliefs show various instruments in use during the Sargonid era. Other, louder instruments were also used. Evidently the soldiers clapped to the rhythm of the music, and maybe even sang along.

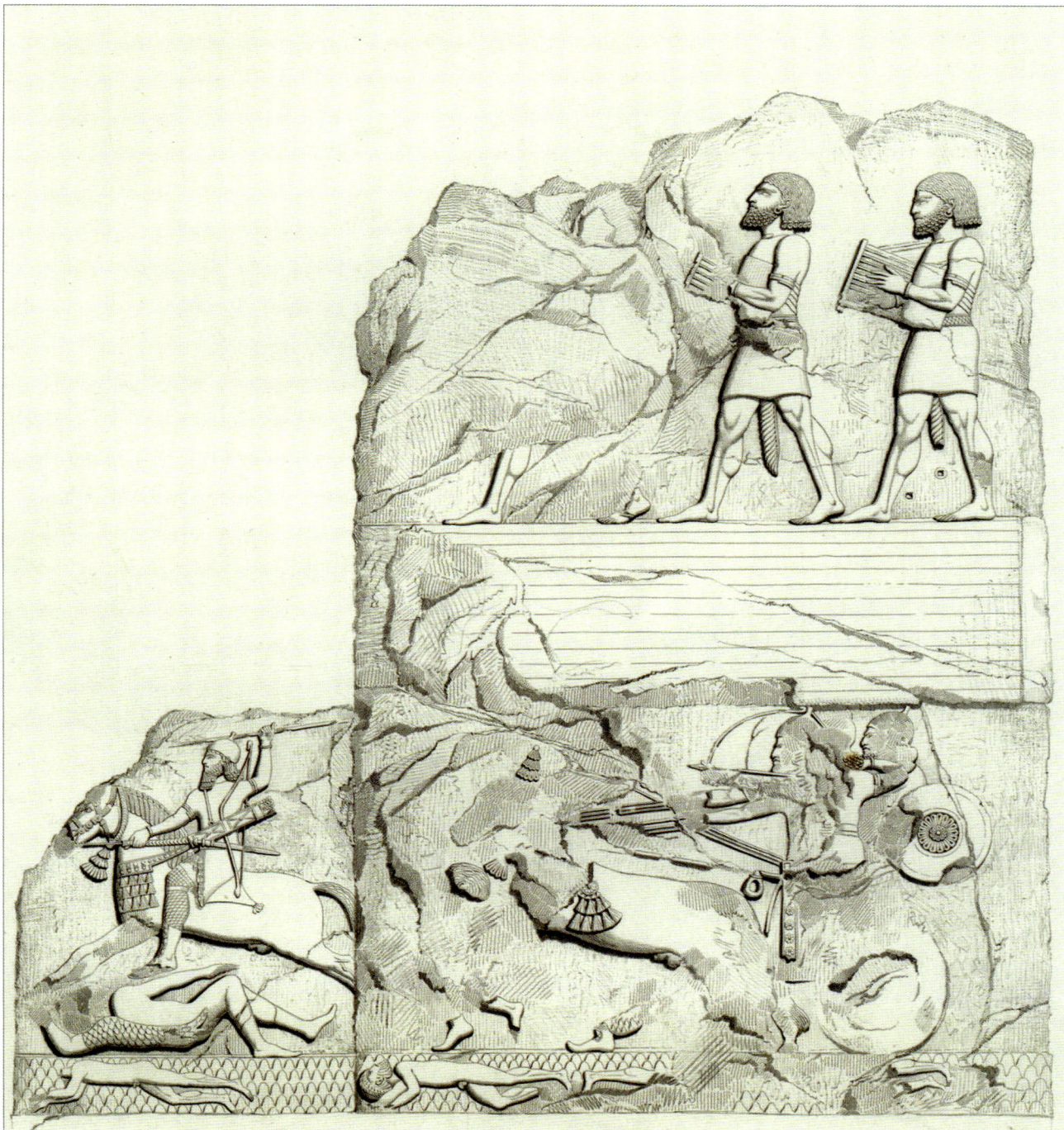

Musicians accompanying an army into battle

Relief from Khorsabad

Paul-Émile Botta, *Monument de Ninive*, vol. 1, plate 67 (page 75).
Digital library, University of Heidelberg.

THE FINAL DAYS OF THE ASSYRIAN EMPIRE –
AN APPROACH TO ITS DECLINE AND FALL

The prophet Isaiah describes the terror of the Israelites in drastic words, and yet foretells the fall of Ashur: *"Woe to the Assyrian, the rod of my anger, in whose hands is the club of my wrath! I send him against a godless nation, I dispatch him against a people who anger me, to seize loot and snatch plunder, and to trample them down like mud in the streets…"* (Isaiah 10, 5).

At the end of the Sargonid era, Assyria's aggressive foreign policy coupled with its demand for unchallenged local supremacy had caused it to become encircled by hostile powers. Some reeled under the scourge of Assyrian occupation hoping for a chance to win back their freedom, while others looked upon Assyria's power with envy. Almost a century of endless campaigning under the Sargonid rulers had wielded the Assyrian army into a battle-hardened and fearsome war machine capable of hammering any enemy who dared challenge it, yet military experience had been bought at the cost of incessant bloodletting. The number of experienced veterans and the sources of Assyrian manpower had gradually been bled white, and the occupation of so vast an empire with its remote garrisons tied down large numbers of troops who would have been better employed elsewhere. The Assyrians had been increasingly forced to recruit ever larger numbers of foreign mercenaries, which made the army altogether less standfast and more unreliable since these men were primarily interested in their own financial gain. Endless deportations had disrupted the traditional ethnic structures of the Assyrian population.

Nevertheless, it took a strong alliance of several foreign powers to finally bring the Assyrian giant to his knees. Apart from the obvious local competitors for supremacy, Media and Babylonia, many other minor powers had their hands in Assyria's fall: Arabs, Arameans, and Scythians all contributed to its demise. Especially the Scythians and Medes were able to provide the enemy alliance with its vital cavalry edge over the dwindling Assyrian forces. The Assyrians were finding themselves assailed by powerful foes on several fronts, and most of these enemies had meanwhile managed to draw even with the Assyrians on a military level. Babylonian general Nabopolassar and Median king Cyaxares, conqueror of the Scythians, were both able tacticians. Nabopolassar, a former high-ranking general in the Babylonian-Assyrian army, rebelled against his royal Assyrian masters. Thus a simple Chaldean noble rose to become the founder of the Neo-Babylonian Empire. Under constant attack from beyond its borders, the Assyrians gradually loosened their grip on the far-flung border provinces. This however resulted in a decreasing amount of tributes on which the Assyrian economy and the especially the army were strongly dependent.

Thus the sheer size of the Neo-Assyrian Empire and its army, its organisation, maintenance, leadership, and the need to maintain stability and cohesion in an essentially multi-ethnic state (if it can thus be called) ultimately posed an insoluble problem even for the most determined and skilled monarch.

Ashurbanipal's royal successors, who did not possess the former's political and strategic talents, were incapable of holding the empire together. The Assyrians found themselves facing powerful opponents whose armies were highly organized, well-equipped, and well-led. Many peoples who had suffered under the Assyrian yoke joined forces with the Babylonians and Medes. To what extent internal strife such as quarrels over the royal succession, local rebellions or famine and disease further contributed to the Assyrian Empire's decline, cannot be said for sure. After the fall of Ashur, the Babylonians marched on to conquer the Levant and Egypt. In his sweep across the Near East, Babylonian king Nebuchadnezzar II destroyed Judah and deported its population, obliterating the last autonomous Jewish kingdom for centuries to come. The Medes conquered the Mannean and Urartean kingdoms. The Medes, a confederation of tribes which had their homelands in the northern and eastern regions of the Zagros mountains, were the overlords of the Persians, another group of tribes living to the south of the Median territory. In 553 BC the Persians, aided by parts of the Median nobility, succeeded in overthrowing their Median overlords and thus laid the foundations of yet another Levantine superpower.

The Babylonian Empire's heyday was short-lived. After the fall of Nineveh, Babylon prospered, especially under the rule of Nabopolassar's son Nebuchadnezzar II. He commissioned the buildings which gave the city such renown in the ancient world, among them the Ishtar Gate with its Processional Way; his architects completed the Etemenanki ziggurat at a time when the crows were already flying among the wind-swept ruins of Assyrian royal cities. Having come to dominate the Medes, the Persians under their king Cyrus II went on to conquer Babylon in 539 BC and quietly incorporated its territory into their own empire. Another oriental high civilisation had thus finally come to an end. The city of Babylon lived on however and was to help usher in the new age of Hellenism. Having defeated the Achaemenids and conquering their realm, Alexander the Great entered the golden city in triumph in 331 BC. His entry marked the beginning of Classic Antiquity.

INDEX OF PERSONS AND PLACE NAMES

BIBLIOGRAPHY

Journals

Der Alte Orient. Gemeinverständliche Darstellungen herausgegeben von der Vorderasiatischen Gesellschaft, J. C. Hinrich'sche Buchhandlung. Leipzig,:
Volume 6 (1905), Issue 3
Weber, Otto: Sanherib. König von Assyrien (705–681)
Volume 11 (1909), Issue 1
Delitzsch, Friedrich: Asurbanipal und die assyrische Kultur seiner Zeit.
Volume 12 (1911), Issue 4
Hunger, Johannes: Heerwesen und Kriegführung der Assyrer auf der Höhe ihrer Macht
Volume 15 (1915)
Meissner, Bruno: Grundzüge der babylonischen und assyrischen Plastik
Volume 20 (1919)
Roeder, Günther: Ägypten und Hethiter

Deutsche Morgenländische Gesellschaft – Zeitschrift für Assyriologie und verwandte Gebiete:
No. 24
Manitius, Walter: Das Stehende Heer der Assyrerkönige und ihre Organisation
No. 34
Meißner, Bruno: Die Eroberung der Stadt Ulhu auf Sargons 8. Feldzug
No. 40
Bauer, Theo: Ein Erstbericht Asarhaddons

Mitteilungen der Deutschen Orientgesellschaft zu Berlin:
No. 115 (Berlin 1983)
Mayer, Walter: Sargons Feldzug gegen Urartu 714 v. Chr.

Die Welt des Orients
No. 38 (2008)
Fuchs, Andreas, Der Turtān Šamši-ilu und die große Zeit der assyrischen Großen (830–746)

Zeitschrift für Assyriologie und Vorderasiatische Archäologie
No. 98 (2008)
Fuchs, Andreas: Über den Wert von Befestigungsanlagen.

Zeitschrift des Deutschen Palästina Vereins
Vol. 2 (Special edition), 1986
Kooij, Arien van der: Das Assyrische Heer vor den Mauern Jerusalems im Jahr 701 v. Chr.

Damals. Das Magazin für Geschichte und Kultur
Vol. 35, Issue 10 (2003)
Fuchs, Andreas: Die Heermassen Assurs.

Zeitschrift für Ägyptologische Forschungen
Vol. 14 (1955)
Zeißl, Helena von: Äthiopier und Assyrer in Ägypten

Books

Andrae, Walter: Das wiedererstandene Assur, Verlag C. H. Beck. Munich, 1977

Archäologie zur Bibel, Kunstschätze aus den biblischen Ländern, Verlag Philipp von Zabern. Mainz, 1981

Ausstellungskatalog der Prähistorischen Staatssammlung Munich, Band 2. 1976

Awdijew, W. I.: Geschichte des Alten Orients, Verlag Volk und Wissen. Berlin, 1953

Barnett, R. D.: Assyrische Skulpturen im British Museum, Verlag Aurel Bongers. Recklinghausen, 1975

Barron, Amy E.: Late Assyrian Arms and Armour: Art versus Artifact, Habilitationsarbeit zum Doktor der Philosophie, University of Toronto. 2010

Bissing, Fr. W. von: Beiträge zur Geschichte der assyrischen Skulptur, in: Abhandlungen der Königlich Bayerischen Akademie der Wissenschaften, Band XXVI, 2. Abhandlung, Verlag der Königlich Bayerischen Akademie der Wissenschaften. Munich, 1912

Bittner, Stefan: Tracht und Bewaffnung des persischen Heeres zur Zeit der Achaimeniden, Verlag Klaus Friedrich. Munich, 1985

Bonnet, Hans: Die Waffen der Völker des alten Orients, J. C. Hinrichs'sche Buchhandlung. Leipzig, 1926

Bonomi, Joseph: Nineveh and its Palaces, Bradbury and Evans. London, 1852

Borchhardt, Jürgen: Homerische Helme, Verlag Philipp von Zabern. Mainz, 1972

Borger, Rykle: Die Inschriften Asarhaddons, Königs von Assyrien, Graz 1956, Neudruck Osnabrück, 1967

Borger, Rykle: Der Bogenköcher im alten Orient, in der Antike und im Alten Testament, in: Nachrichten der Akademie der Wissenschaften in Göttingen, Vandenhoeck & Ruprecht. Göttingen, 2000

Born, Hermann; Steidl, Ursula: Schutzwaffen aus Assyrien und Urartu, Sammlung Axel Guttmann, Verlag Philipp von Zabern. Mainz, 1995

Botta, Paul-Èmile: Monument de Ninive Teil 1–5, J. Baudry, Editeurs. Paris, 1847–1850

Brentjes, Burchard: Land zwischen den Strömen, Koehler & Amelang. Leipzig, 1963

Brentjes, Burchard: Drei Jahrtausende Armenien, Koehler & Amelang. Leipzig, 1973

Brentjes, Burchard: Völker am Euphrat und Tigris, Koehler & Amelang. Leipzig, 1981

Calmeyer, Peter (Hrsg.): Beiträge zur altorientalischen Archäologie und Altertumskunde: Festschrift für Barthel Hrouda zum 65. Geburtstag, Harrassowitz. Wiesbaden, 1994

Ceram, C. W.: Götter, Gräber und Gelehrte im Bild, Bertelsmann Verlag. Gütersloh, 1962

Ceram, C. W.: Götter Gräber und Gelehrte, Roman der Archäologie, Verlag Volk und Welt. Berlin, 1980

Çilingiroğlu, Altan: Die Geschichte des Königreiches Van Urartu, Ofis Ticaret Matbaacilik Ltd. Izmir, 1988

Curtis, John: An Examination of Late Assyrian Metalwork with special reference to Nimrud, Oxbow Books. Oxford, 2013

Das Gold der Steppe, Archäologie der Ukraine, Ausstellung im Schloss Gottorf, Archäologisches Landesmuseum Schleswig. Schleswig, 1991

De Backer, Fabrice: The Neo-Assyrian Shield, Lockwood Press. Atlanta, 2016

Delitzsch, Friedrich: Die Babylonische Chronik, Verlag B. G. Teubner. Leipzig, 1906

Demmin, August: Die Kriegswaffen in ihrer geschichtlichen Entwickelung von den ältesten Zeiten bis auf die Gegenwart, Verlag P. Friesenhahn. Leipzig, 1893

Die Hethiter und Ihr Reich, Kunst- und Ausstellungshalle der Bundesrepublik Deutschland, Konrad Theiss Verlag GmbH. Stuttgart, 2002

Dothan, Trude und Moshe: Die Philister, Eugen Diederichs Verlag. Munich, 1995

Dezsö, Tamás; Curtis, John: Assyrian Iron Helmerts from Nimrud, now in the British Museum, in Zeitschrift Iraq 53 (1991)

Dezsö, Tamás: The Assyrian Army, I. Structure of the Neo-Assyrian Army, 1. Infantry, Eötvós Loród University Press. Budapest, 2012

Dezsö, Tamás: The Assyrian Army, I. Structure of the Neo-Assyrian Army, 2. Cavalry and Chariotry, Eötvós Loród University Press. Budapest, 2012

Dezsö, Tamás The Assyrian Army, II. Recruitment and Logistics, Eötvós Loród University Press. Budapest, 2016

Falck, Martin von; Petschel, Susanne, (Hrsg.), Pharao siegt immer, Krieg und Frieden im Alten Ägypten, Druck Verlag Kettler. Bönen, 2004

Fuchs, Andreas: Die Annalen des Jahres 711 v. Chr. nach Prismenfragmenten in Ninive und Assur, State Archives of Assyria Studies, vol. 8. Helsinki, 1998

Fuchs, Andreas: War das neuassyrische Reich ein Militärstaat? Originalveröffentlichung in: Meißner, B.; Schmidt, O.; Sommer, M. (Hrsg.) in: Krieg-Gesellschaft-Institutionen. Beiträge zu einer vergleichenden Kriegsgeschichte, Akademie Verlag. Berlin, 2005

Fuchs, Andreas: Gyges, Assurbanipal und Dugdamme/Lygdamis: Absurde Kontakte zwischen Anatolien und Ninive in: Rollinger Robert (Hrsg.), Interkulturalität in der Alten Welt. Wiesbaden, 2010

Fuchs, Andreas: Die Inschriften Sargons II. aus Khorsabad, Cuvillier Verlag. Göttingen, 1994

Fuchs, Andreas, Borger, Rykle: Beiträge zum Inschriftenwerk Assurbanipals, Otto Harrassowitz Verlag. Wiesbaden, 1996

Galter, D. Hannes: Vom Streitwagen zur Reiterei, in: Dornik, Wolfram; Gießauf, Johannes; Walter M. (Hrsg.): Krieg und Wirtschaft von der Antike bis ins 21. Jahrhundert, Studien Verlag. Innsbruck, 2010

Gestermann, Louise: Die Plünderung Thebens durch assyrische Truppen – Eine Randbemerkung aus ägyptologischer Sicht, Hallesche Beiträge zur Orientwissenschaft 29. Halle, 2000

Gless, Karlheinz: Das Pferd im Militärwesen, Militärverlag der DDR. Berlin, 1980

Gressmann, Hugo: Altorientalische Texte zum Alten Testament, Verlag Walter de Gruyter & Co. Berlin. Leipzig, 1926

Gressmann, Hugo: Altorientalische Bilder zum Alten Testament, Verlag Walter de Gruyter & Co. Berlin. Leipzig, 1927

Gundlach, Rolf; Vogel, Carola: Militärgeschichte des pharaonischen Ägypten. Altägypten und seine Nachbarkulturen im Spiegel aktueller Forschung, Ferdinand Schöningh. Paderborn, 2009

Halama, Simon Moritz: Assyrische und babylonische Festungen des ersten Jahrtausends v. Chr. in ihrem Kontext, Magisterarbeit am Institut für Vorderasiatische Archäologie, Orientalisches Seminar der Albert-Ludwigs-Universität. Freiburg, 2006

Healy, Marc: The Ancient Assyrians, Elite Series Nr. 39, Osprey Publishing Ltd. Oxford, 1991

Herrmann, Siegfried: Geschichte Israels in alttestamentarischer Zeit, Evangelische Verlagsanstalten. Berlin, 1981

Herm, Gerhard: Die Phönizier, Econ Verlag. Düsseldorf/Vienna, 1973

Hinz, Walther: Das Reich Elam, W. Kohlhammer Verlag. Stuttgart, 1964

Hirschberg, Hans: Studien zur Geschichte Esarhaddons, König von Assyrien (681–669), Verlag Dr. H. Eschenhagen. Ohlau, 1932

Horn, Valentin: Das Pferd im Alten Orient, in: Documenta Hippologica Olms Presse Hildesheim. Zürich, New York, 1995

Housten, Mary G.: Ancient Egyptian, Mesopotamian and Persian Costume, Dover Publications, Inc. Mineola. New York, 2002

Hottenroth, Friedrich: Trachten Haus,- Feld- und Kriegsgeräthschaften der Völker alter und neuer Zeit, Teil 1 und 2, Verlag G. Weise. Stuttgart, 1884–1891

Hrouda, Barthel: Der Alte Orient, C. Bertelsmann Verlag GmbH. Munich, 1991

Hrouda, Barthel: Der Assyrische Streitwagen, in: Iraq Vol. 25, Nr. 2, British Institute for the Study of Iraq (Hrsg.), 1963

Keller, Werner: Und die Bibel hat doch Recht, Naumann & Göbel Verlagsgesellschaft mbH. Cologne, 1989

Kellner, Hans-Jörg: Bemerkungen zu den Helmen in Urartu, in: Anadolu Araştırmaları – Anatolian Research 8. Istanbul, 1980

Kellner, Hans-Jörg: Urartu, ein wiederentdeckter Rivale Assyriens,

Klengel-Brandt, Evelyn: Die Herrscher von Assur, Verlag Philipp von Zabern. Mainz, 2005

Klengel, Horst: Syria Antiqua, Edition Leipzig 1971

Knudtzon, J. A.: Assyrische Gebete an den Sonnengott für Staat und königliches Haus aus der Zeit Asarhaddons und Assurbanipals, Band II, Verlag Eduard Pfeiffer. Leipzig, 1893

Lau, Robert J.: The Annals of Ashurbanapal (v. Rawlinson pl. 1–10), Buchhandlung und Druckerei E. J. Brill. Leiden, 1903

Layard, Austen Henry: The Monuments of Nineveh, John Murray. London, 1849

Layard, Austen Henry: A Second Series of the Monuments of Nineveh, John Murray. London, 1853

Layard, Austen Henry: Discoveries in the Ruins of Ninive and Babylon, Harper & Brothers, Publishers. New York, 1853

Luschan, Felix von: Ausgrabungen in Sendschirli, Verlag von Georg Reimer. Berlin, 1911

Lyon, D. G.: Keilschrifttexte Sargon`s, Königs von Assyrien, J. C. Hinrichs'sche Buchhandlung. Leipzig, 1883

Magall, Miriam: Archäologie und Bibel, DuMont Buchverlag. Cologne, 1986

Maspero, Gustave: Ägypten und Assyrien, B. G. Teubner Verlag. Leipzig, 1891

Maspero, Gustave: Struggles of the Nations - Egypt, Syria and Assyria. London, 1896

Mayer, Walter: Sargons Feldzug gegen Urartu 714 v. Chr. – Eine militärische Würdigung, in Mitteilungen der Deutschen Orientgesellschaft Berlin, Nr. 112. Berlin, 1980

Mayer, Walter: Gedanken zum Einsatz von Streitwagen, in: Ugarit-Forschungen, Jahrgang 1978, Band 10, in Internationales Jahrbuch für die Altertumskunde Syrien-Palästinas

Mayer, Walter: Politik und Kriegskunst der Assyrer, Ugarit-Verlag. Münster, 1995

Meißner, Burkhard; Schmitt, Oliver; Sommer, Michael (Hrsg.): Krieg-Gesellschaft-Institutionen, Beiträge zu einer vergleichenden Kriegsgeschichte, darin Fuchs, Andreas: War Assyrien ein Militärstaat?. Berlin, 2005

Moortgat, Anton: Alt-Vorderasiatische Malerei, Safari-Verlag Carl Boldt und Reinhard Jaspert. Berlin, 1959

Moortgat, Anton: Die Kunst des Alten Mesopotamien, DuMont Buchverlag. Cologne, 1984

Nagel, Gottfried Johannes Samuel: Der Zug des Sanherib gegen Jerusalem, J. C. Hinrichs'sche Buchhandlung. Leipzig, 1902

Nagel, Wolfram: Der mesopotamische Streitwagen und seine Entwicklung im ostmediterranen Bereich, Verlag Bruno Hessling. Berlin, 1966

Nagel, Wolfram: Die neuassyrischen Reliefstile unter Sanherib und Assurbanaplu, in: Berliner Beiträge zur Vor- und Frühgeschichte, Band 11, Verlag Bruno Hessling. Berlin, 1967

Naue, Julius: Die vorrömischen Schwerter aus Kupfer, Bronze und Eisen, Verlag Piloty & Loehle. Munich, 1903

Newman, John, P.: The Thrones and Palaces of Babylon and Nineveh, Harper & Brothers. Washington, 1875

Onasch, Hans-Ulrich: Die assyrischen Eroberungen Ägyptens, in: Zeitschrift Ägypten und Altes Testament Nr. 27, Harrassowitz Verlag. Wiesbaden, 1994

Pancritius, Marie, Charlotte: Assyrische Kriegsführung von Tiglat-pileser I. bis auf Šamši-Adad III., Inaugural-Dissertation, Hartungsche Buchhandlung. Königsberg, 1904

Parrot, André: Assur, Librairie Gallimard. Paris, 1961

Pelizaeus-Museum Hildesheim, Die Ägyptische Sammlung, Verlag Philipp von Zabern. Mainz, 1993

Pjotrowski, Boris: Urartu, Wilhelm Heyne Verlag. Munich, 1980

Place, Victor: Ninive et l'Assyrie, Tome Troisiéme Planches. Paris, 1867

Pongratz-Leisten, B.; Deller, K.; Bleibtreu, E.: Götterstreitwagen und Götterstandarten, in: Baghdader Mitteilungen Nr. 23, Jahrgang 1992, Deutsches Archäologisches Institut Abteilung Baghdad

Prisse d'Avennes, Èmile,: Egyptian Art, Verlag Taschen. Cologne, 2014

Rasin, J. A.: Geschichte der Kriegskunst, Band 1, Die Kriegskunst der Sklavenhalterperiode des Krieges, Verlag des Ministeriums für Nationale Verteidigung der DDR. Berlin, 1959

Reade, Julian: Assyrian Sculpture, British Museum Publications. London, 1986

Rehm, Ellen: Kykladen und Alter Orient, Bestandskatalog des Badischen Landesmuseum Karlsruhe, G. Braun Printconsult GmbH. Karlsruhe, 1997

Reimpell, Walter: Geschichte der assyrischen und babylonischen Kleidung, Verlag Karl Curtius. Berlin, 1921

Rolle, Renate; Müller-Wille, Michael; Schietzel, Kurt (Hrsg.): Gold der Steppe, Archäologie der Ukraine, Ausstellungskatalog des Archäologischen Landesmuseum Schleswig. Schleswig, 1991

Schertler, Otto; Lunyakov, Sascha: Die Heere im Alten Orient, in: Heere und Waffen Nr. 8, Zeughaus Verlag. Berlin, 2010

Schiffer, Sina jun.: Die Aramäer. Gütersloh, 1992

Schmidtke, Friedrich: Die Statthalterschaft Asarhaddons und seine Thronbesteigung in Assyrien 681 v. Chr., - Inaugural-Dissertation, Buchhandlung und Druckerei E. J. Brill. Leiden, 1916

Schipper, Bernd Ulrich: Israel und Ägypten in der Königszeit. Die kulturellen Kontakte von Salomo bis zum Fall Jerusalems, Universitätsverlag Freiburg Schweiz; Vandenhoeck & Ruprecht. Göttingen, 1999

Scholtz, Richard: Das Ischtar-Tor und die Prozessionsstraße von Babylon ein geschichtlicher Überblick und die Anleitung zum Bau eines Zinnfigurendioramas und Levec, Manfred (zusammengestellt): Ein Leitfaden für Zinnfigurensammler, Kostümsammler etc. der babylonisch/assyrischen Epoche von Otto Gottstein. London,, Major Otto Müller. Berlin,, Prof. Paul Coiussin, Marseille, Selbstverlag. Stuttgart

Schrader, Eberhard: Die Sargonstele des Berliner Museums, Abhandlungen der königlichen Akademie der Wissenschaften. Berlin, 1882

Scurlock, Ann: Neo Assyrian Battle Tactics, CDL Press, Bethesda. Maryland, 1997

Smith, Samuel Alden: Die Keilschrifttexte Asurbanipals, Königs von Assyrien (668–626 v. Chr.), Verlag Eduard Pfeiffer. Leipzig, 1887

Streck, Maximilian: Assurbanipal und die letzten Assyrischen Könige bis zum Untergange Ninive`s, 3 Bände. C. Hinrichs'sche Buchhandlung. Leipzig, 1916

Unger, Eckhard: Zum Bronzetor von Balawat, Beiträge zur Erklärung und Deutung der assyrischen Inschriften und Reliefs Salmanassars III., Verlag Eduard Pfeiffer. Leipzig, 1913

Velikovsky, Immanuel: Die Seevölker, Umschau Verlag Breitenstein. Frankfurt am Main, 1978

Wallis, Ernst: Illustrerad Verldshistoria, Chicago 1894

Wartke, Bernhard Ralf: Urartu, das Reich am Ararat, Verlag Philipp von Zabern. Mainz, 1993

Wegner, Max: Die Musikinstrumente des Alten Orients, Aschendorffsche Verlagsbuchhandlung. Münster, 1950

Weissbach, Friedrich Heinrich, Die Denkmäler und Inschriften an der Mündung des Nahr el-Kelb, Verlag Walter de Gruyter. Berlin und Leipzig, 1922

Wicke, Dirk: Neuassyrische Schuppenpanzer und ein Neufund in Ziyaret Tepe, Kaniuth, Kai; Lau, Daniel; Wicke, Dirk (Hrsg.), in: Übergangszeiten, Altorientalische Studien für Reinhard Dittmann anlässlich seines 65. Geburtstags, Zaphon. Münster, 2018

Winckler, Hugo, Geschichte Babyloniens und Assyriens,Verlag Eduard Pfeiffer. Leipzig, 1892

Roland Sennewald

The Enemies of the Assyrian Sargonid Empire

Urartean, Elamite, Israelite, Aramean, Philistine, Phoenician, Babylonian, Median, Cimmerian, Mannaean and other armies.

This volume will follow up the book on Neo-Assyrian armies under the Sargonid dynasty. Well-known enemies and allies of the Assyrian Empire such as the Egyptians, Scythians, Arabs, Early Greeks and Persians will be discussed as will the armies of lesser-known kingdoms and states which challenged the power of Assyria. The book will again be chiefly based on the available archaeological evidence.

Photographs of reconstructions and original finds will again be supplemented by colour plates by artist Stefano Borin which will bring to life dress, equipment and appearance of these ancient warriors of the Near East. It will be revealed that despite the Assyrians' ability to maintain political and military dominance in the region, their power did by no means go unchallenged. Tactics and equipment enabled numerous enemies of the Sargonids to hold their ground against Assyrian armies, and victories were often enough mixed with reverses.

However, it was not the advanced and highly organized kingdoms of Urartu and Elam which ultimately brought about the downfall of the Assyrian Empire but the warlike horsemen of the Scythians and Medes, who allied themselves with the Babylonians. Years of war comprising the conquest of new territories from the mountains to the deserts of Sudan, the quelling of rebellions, and fighting against invaders as diverse as Arab raiders and Cimmerian nomad warriors had finally exhausted Assyrian resources. The mighty empire staggered and fell under the attacks of the multiple enemies by which it was surrounded.

The book will appear in 2023.